Wumi Raji

# Long Dreams in Short Chapters

# African Languages – African Literatures
# Langues Africaines – Littératures Africaines

Volume 2

LIT

Wumi Raji

# Long Dreams in Short Chapters

## Essays in African Postcolonial Literary, Cultural and Political Criticisms

LIT

Cover design by Kawahay Daniel, Maiduguri.
Photo by Peter Steigerwald, Frobenius Institut, Frankfurt.

**Bibliographic information published by the Deutsche Nationalbibliothek**
The Deutsche Nationalbibliothek lists this publication in the Deutsche Nationalbibliografie; detailed bibliographic data are available in the Internet at http://dnb.d-nb.de.

ISBN 978-3-8258-1841-8

**A catalogue record for this book is available from the British Library**



Fresnostr. 2 D-48159 Münster
Tel. +49 (0) 2 51-620 32 22 Fax +49 (0) 2 51-922 60 99
e-Mail: lit@lit-verlag.de http://www.lit-verlag.de

**Distribution:**
In Germany: LIT Verlag Fresnostr. 2, D-48159 Münster
Tel. +49 (0) 2 51-620 32 22, Fax +49 (0) 2 51-922 60 99, e-Mail: vertrieb@lit-verlag.de

In Austria: Medienlogistik Pichler-ÖBZ GmbH & Co KG
IZ-NÖ, Süd, Straße 1, Objekt 34, A-2355 Wiener Neudorf
Tel. +43 (0) 22 36-63 53 52 90, Fax +43 (0) 22 36-63 53 52 43, e-Mail: mlo@medien-logistik.at

In Switzerland: B + M Buch- und Medienvertriebs AG
Hochstr. 357, CH-8200 Schaffhausen
Tel. +41 (0) 52-643 54 30, Fax +41 (0) 52-643 54 35, e-Mail: order@buch-medien.ch

In the UK by: Global Book Marketing, 99B Wallis Rd, London, E9 5LN
Phone: +44 (0) 20 8533 5800 – Fax: +44 (0) 1600 775 663
http://www.centralbooks.co.uk/html

In North America by:

Transaction Publishers
New Brunswick (U.S.A.) and London (U.K.)

Transaction Publishers
Rutgers University
35 Berrue Circle
Piscataway, NJ 08854

Phone: +1 (732) 445 - 2280
Fax: + 1 (732) 445 - 3138
for orders (U. S. only):
toll free (888) 999 - 6778
e-mail: orders@transactionpub.com

TO:

I

My colleagues and compatriots at the University of Ilorin, Nigeria, unjustly sacked between 2000 and 2001. I offer this as part of the struggle.

II

Dipo Fashina and Edwin Madunagu

For the principles they stand for, the examples they set and the inspirations they provide.

III

Professor Oyin Ogunba (In memoriam)

For stretching out a hand of assistance when it really mattered.

## Special Acknowledgment

I would like to express an appreciation to the Alexander von Humboldt Foundation, Bonn, Germany for the generous sponsorship it provided toward the publication of this book.

# Acknowledgments

I am grateful to the Alexander von Humboldt Foundation for the fellowships utilized at the University of Bayreuth, Germany between August 2000 and October 2001; and the Technical University of Dresden between April and September 2002 during which periods most of the essays in this book were either first drafted and/or presented or, on the other hand, revised for publication. I thank Eckhard Breitinger, my host Professor at the University of Bayreuth whose publication outfit – the Bayreuth African Studies Series (BASS) constitutes the subject of chapter nine of the book. I have very fond memories of my different periods of stay at the Technical University of Dresden. Uwe Boeker, my host Professor, not only provided me with an environment that is very conducive for research, he also made out time to attend to the details of my personal needs. I am exceedingly grateful to him for this and many more – including, for example, the numerous letters of recommendation that he has had to write for me over the years. I must also mention it that Uwe it was who first suggested the idea of doing something on Wole Soyinka's *Opera Wonyosi*, the African Nobel laureate's composite adaptation of John Gay's *The Beggars' Opera* and Bertolt Brecht's *The Three penny Opera*, and he published the resulting essay in John Gay's *The Three penny Opera: Adaptations and Re-Writings* which he edited jointly with Ines Detmers and Anna Christina Giovanopoulous. "Opera Wonyosi: Strategies of a Postcolonial Response to a European Operatic Drama," being the title of the essay in question, now represents the opening chapter of this book. I thank him for making the original suggestion. I thank Professor Olu Ashaolu, my doctoral supervisor at the University of Ibadan, and Professor Harry Garuba (now of the University of Cape Town, South Africa) who advised me informally on the same work for their overall contributions to my intellectual career.

My peregrinations in the last eight years have taken me to several countries in Africa and the Western world and I encountered a lot of wonderful people on the way. I would like to thank Nina Klinge – Nygard, programme officer of the Nordic Africa Institute, Sweden and Mai Palmberg coordinator of the Cultural Images in and of Africa project for making my short stay at the institute in 2003 a wonderful experience. Nina was one of the very few people to which I revealed the story of my problem with the University of Ilorin. She not only kept the story to herself, she also made sure that her knowledge of my status as an unemployed person did not affect her attitude towards me. I thank her for being so reliable and trustworthy. I would also like to thank John Stotesbury and Raisa Simola of the University of Joensuu, Finland and Kirsten Holst – Peterson of Roskilde University, Denmark. I met the three of them in the course of my tour of the Nordic countries and I cherish the friendship that I have established with them. Oladele Oyelakin, Lamin Sidibe and Ramatoulaye Guisse made the brief period I spent at the University of The Gambia a remarkable experience. I am grateful to the three of them. I would also like to thank Lansana Juwara whom I had earlier run into in Sweden and through whom I met Lena Sawyer. Lena was later to play a crucial role at a critical time in the life of my family. I continue to remember this.

My appreciation goes to Maria Olaussen of Vaxjo University, Sweden. Maria is the initiator of Africa Writing Europe project. It was a great inspiration working with her on this project, and the three months I spent in her University in 2005 were quite memorable. It was delightful working with the members of the research team she put together as well. In particular, I would like to thank Christina Angelfors of the same Vaxjo University, Dorothy Driver of the University of Adelaide, Australia, Gabeba Baderoon of Penn State University, USA, Geoffrey Davis of the Technical University of Aachen, Germany and Veronique Bonnet of the University of Paris XIII, France. I thank Hilary Dannenberg of the University of Bayreuth for the guest professorship of April/May, 2007, and the support she has continued to provide since then. I was a visiting research fellow at the University of Cambridge, UK between October 2006 and March 2007. I thank Derek Peterson, the director of the Centre of African Studies for the invitation, Richard Drayton, who served as my adviser during the visit and Dorian Addison, the Centre's administrator.

It is important for me to express appreciation to all those who have identified with me in the ordeal that I have been going through since the last eight years. They are too numerous to list out; I know. All the same, I would like to put on record my feelings of appreciation for the moral, political and/or material support extended to me by such people as Professor Biodun Jeyifo, Professor Tanure Ojaide, Professor Tejumola Olaniyan, Dr. Omofolabo Ajayi – Soyinka, Dr. Kola Babarinde, Akin Adesokan, Ogaga Ifowodo, Pius Adesanmi, Sola Olorunyomi, Ademola Dasylva, Hakeem Bello, Yomi Adegbamigbe and Niyi Okunoye. Professor Niyi Osundare is a friend, uncle and brother all rolled into one, and so is Odia Ofeimun. My gratitude to both of them. To fellow victims of the tyrannical administration at the University of Ilorin; but especially to Professors Oduleye and Akinyanju, Taiwo Oloruntoba – Oju, Yinka Banwo, Yetunde Osunfisan, Debo Ajayi, Tayo Oloruntoba – Oju and Femi Dunmade, I say we shall triumph in the end. To Gabriel Otsemobor who gave me his laptop when mine packed up while preparing the final version of the manuscript of this book, I give my gratitude as well.

But how do I begin to thank members of my immediate family? Romoke, my wife, Yebosayo, my daughter, and Yasir and Oluwaniyi, my two sons have all stood by me in these years of profound crisis. We have all borne the humiliation, and endured the deprivations, together. Even now, we still remain separated – with them located on one side of the Atlantic and me on another; and the two parties visiting each other only occasionally. Here is hoping that someday or sometime, I will be able to reciprocate the understanding, devotion and love they have shown, and which they continue to demonstrate.

# TABLE OF CONTENTS

# PREFACE

"What you have just seen is a short chapter in a l-o-n-g dream"[1]

Individually, the essays published together in this book were, in the main, written during a period of intense crisis in my life and career; and I consider the moment of publishing them together in a single volume the auspicious time for setting the story down on record.

My ordeal began when I won the Alexander von Humboldt research fellowship, awarded by a foundation of the same name, based in Bonn, Germany in early 2000. The formal letter of award of the fellowship came to hand on February 7 of that year and immediately on February 8, I forwarded a letter to the University of Ilorin, my employers at the time, applying for a leave to utilize the award. The application was strongly supported by the Head of my Department and, also, the Dean of my Faculty. For over a month after sending the letter, I received no word from the University administration. And on March 13, when it had become clear that the Appointment and Promotions Committee, the statutory body saddled with the responsibility of taking decisions on such matters would not be able to meet before March 29, my scheduled date of departure, I forwarded another letter addressed, this time, to the Vice-Chancellor requesting for executive approval of my application for leave. Again, the letter received the express support both of the Head of my Department and the Dean of the Faculty of Arts. After submitting the application, I made several attempts to see the Vice-Chancellor but all were in vain. Thus it happened that on March 29, 2000, my Head of Department and the Dean of the Faculty took a joint decision to release me to proceed on my fellowship, pending the time my application would be finally approved.

What the administration did as soon as it learned that I had left the country was to order the Bursary Department to stop my salary with immediate effect. It also issued me a query dated May 4, 2000 and sent it to my Department in Ilorin, even while demonstrating in it an awareness of the fact that I was already in Germany. Thereafter, the same administration proceeded to arraign me before the Staff Disciplinary and Appeals Committee in absentia and on December 19, 2000, I received in Bayreuth, Germany, a letter sent via DHL by the University administration, ordering me to return to my duty post in Ilorin, Nigeria, unfailingly on December 21, 2000.

---

[1] Niyi Osundare, *The State Visit*. (Ibadan: Kraftgriots, 2002): 64

On receiving this letter, I immediately wrote back to the Governing Council of the University explaining my inability to meet the deadline since I would need time to wind up my research, notify the Alexander von Humboldt Foundation that awarded me the fellowship of my intention to cut short the period of my stay, think of a proper way to evacuate my family and, perhaps most importantly, raise the fare for the flight back to Nigeria. To my dismay, the next letter I received from the University simply informed me of a summary termination of my appointment for "having failed to return to your duty post as at 21st December, 2000." Again, I wrote another letter dated January 25, 2001 and addressed to the same Governing Council pleading for a reconsideration of my case but the University simply responded by stating that it had found no reason upon which to base a review of my case. This is the beginning of my troubles and they continued till I secured my current appointment at the Obafemi Awolowo University, Ile Ife.

My case as well as those of over fifty others who were sacked under similar circumstances by the same administration is a minor incident when considered against the enormity of the problems confronting Nigeria, indeed most countries of postcolonial Africa, but it is part of the problems all the same. Most nations on the continent are simply in the grip of cynical and extremely cruel people – individuals who, absolutely, have no respect for basic human rights and the rule of law, who continue to subject the peoples of their different countries to unimaginable brutalities and oppression, who indulge in shamefaced corruption, and who, in short, perpetrate mindless authoritarianism and maintain a very frightening form of autocratic control on the citizenry. The history of the crisis dates far back in years and it links up with colonial experience and the attitudes of those who took over the political leadership of the new African nations following independence.

In *You must set forth at Dawn*; Wole Soyinka gave an account of his experience with some of those nationalists while he was a student in Britain in the 1950s. As the first African Nobel prize winner in literature makes clear in his autobiographical work, the attitudes of these people simply portrayed them as those without any sense of responsibility, and with absolutely lack of concern for the fates of the nations and peoples whose causes they were supposed to have flown to Britain to pursue. Soyinka writes of these people's total alienation, their utter emptiness, and paints a graphic picture of, to use his exact words, "their self – preening, their ostentatious spending, their cultivated condescension, (and) even disdain towards the people they were supposed to represent." [2] There were exceptions, of course, and Soyinka makes this clear. These ones invited the young students to serious talks where they laid out the details of their plans for the future of their countries. These were few, very few, and it is important to emphasize

[2] Wole Soyinka, *You must set Forth at Dawn*. (Ibadan: Bookcraft, 2006): 48

this point. As for the others, their respective nations were no more than "prostrate victim(s)," again as Soyinka puts it, available to be ravished at will. Summing up, the Nobel winning writer likens the people to "flamboyant replacements of the old colonial order, not transforming agents, not even empathizing participants in a process of liberation." [3]

The words may be harsh but the assessments appear to be totally accurate, in my view. It indeed bears no repeating the details of the crimes that those who took over the reigns of leadership at independence perpetrated against their own people – the culture of corruption they fostered, the squander-mania they indulged in, the acts of repression they perpetrated, the dictatorship they foisted on the people, etc. The consequences, of course, were the military coups that occurred in most of these countries within the first ten years of their existence as independent nations. Again, this is well known. And it is common knowledge as well that in the specific case of Nigeria, the manner of the execution of the first coup carried out in January 1966 precipitated a civil war which, luckily, the country survived. Following this was a period of oil boom, but the country's ruling elites, rather than use the proceeds for the development of the land and its peoples, have continued to behave like a group of hens surrounding a calabash of corn – gorging themselves! Once a handful of people continue to monopolize the resources of the nation, the rest of the citizenry is bound to become desperate. This has been the case with Nigeria, and the discontent has been manifested through all kinds of crises, principal among which are religious and ethno – nationalist strives.

In other countries like Uganda, Congo Kinshasa, Equatorial Guinea and Central African Republic, the military dictators who hijacked powers immediately after the attainment of independence simply transformed themselves into emperors and/or presidents – for – life. And they released their hold on power only after it had become absolutely impossible for them to continue to stay on, after they had foisted crises of profound proportions on their different countries, crises which many of them have not yet emerged from, even now. In Zimbabwe, continued domination by white settlers constituting only a fraction of the population was eventually battled down in 1980 through popular struggle. The irony of the whole thing however, is that Robert Mugabe who led the liberation struggle and who became the country's popular leader at independence has, in the end, turned out to be a terrible contradiction and the result is the profound crisis in which his country is deeply mired.

The question may then be asked: what has all this got to do with the issues explored in this book? In response to this hypothetical question, I return a one – word answer: everything. The adjective "postcolonial" in the second part of the

---

[3] *You must set Forth at Dawn*, 48

title of this book, and as is well – known, once applied to qualify literature, culture, theatre or any other art forms, often implies the engagement in the respective discipline(s) of the historical developments leading to, and following, the attainment of formal independence in formerly colonized countries. Postcolonialism can be ambivalent, in which case it will be concerned mainly with the exploration of the areas of intersections and convergences in the identities and cultures of the peoples of the societies of the metropolis and those of the emergent ones of the peripheries while at the same time equivocating on the other important consequences of the historical encounter between these societies. It can, on the other hand, be positioned on the side of the subject peoples. While not, of course, ignoring the complicated connections and intricate relationships that have generated over the years between the peoples of the centre and those of the periphery of the world's social formations, this version of postcolonialism nonetheless concerns itself with the question of restoring agencies to the "historically vanquished" of the world. The quoted words belong specifically to Elleke Boehmer. In the short afterword she published along with the 2005 edition of her *Colonial and Postcolonial Literature*, Boehmer makes it clear how, while maintaining continuous vigilance against new forms of colonial control, the practitioners of this second category of postcolonialism concern themselves more with the particular contradictions and conflicts of their specific places and periods. It is in this particular regard, and as Boehmer further argues, that different postcolonial writers and cultural workers have continued to "undercut anything resembling a universal or transnational category of postcolonial… aesthetic; (and) troubled the homogenization of hybridity and migrancy as trans-cultural, universally form – giving conditions." [4]

The subjects of most of the chapters in this book belong broadly in this second category of postcolonialism. In their expressions and attitudes, they betray a passionate identification with the fate of the peoples of the different countries of postcolonial Africa. To them, the continent is not a single, borderless constituency but, rather, a profoundly heterogeneous space. In spite of this however, they still make sure to avoid political and/or cultural parochialism in their individual projects. Some participate actively in the struggles directed at refashioning the identities of the peoples of their immediate localities but it is often certain that what they do have relevance for similar contexts and situations both in Africa and other parts of the developing world. This is especially true of Wole Soyinka and the late Ken Saro – Wiwa. Femi Osofisan, Niyi Osundare (who, otherwise, is better known as a poet) and Akanji Nasiru work, again like Wole Soyinka, in the theatre. In their different works, they recuperate forgotten archives, imbuing them with fresh, transformative interpretations. Nasiru's work studied here was a com-

[4] Elleke Boehmer, *Colonial and Postcolonial Literature*. (Oxford: Oxford University Press): 250

missioned project, part of a campaign aimed at generating awareness on maternal mortality. It was sponsored by the World Health Organisation.

Dambudzo Marechera is undoubtedly positioned in the interstitial zone of postcolonialism. His identity as a writer is that of one who inhabits the liminal space between the periphery and the metropolis and his works studied here demonstrate clearly the ambiguities and contradictions that characterise both his life and writings. The first part of the chapter on him however articulates an alternative perspective of cultural identity for postcolonial Africa. This indeed is a subject that I plan to return to in future studies.

On his own, Eckhard Breitinger is a citizen of the metropolis but his publishing project studied in chapter nine of the book appears to be devoted to the rejuvenation of the hopes and aspirations of a number of African intellectual workers disadvantaged because of their locations.

But to round off on this preface, it is what I have perceived as most of my subjects' anthem for the marginalized citizens of postcolonial Africa that I have described in the title of this book as "long dreams." The expression itself is not original to me as can be seen in the epigraph to this preface. What I have done, merely, is to paraphrase a statement in the winding – up comments of Niyi Osundare's narrator in his *The State Visit* studied in chapter seven of this book. What this means then is that I see the writers, dramatists and culture workers that constitute the focus of this study as trying to grapple with different kinds of dreams – different kinds of visions for the different peoples of the African periphery; and my efforts in the book simply serves as an attempt at apprehending these dreams as well as the strategies deployed in articulating them.

# Part I

# Postcolonial: The Literary…

# CHAPTER 1

# OPERA WONYOSI: STRATEGIES OF A POSTCOLONIAL RESPONSE TO A WESTERN OPERATIC DRAMA [1]

## I. WOLE SOYINKA, DRAMATIST AND CRITIC OF SOCIETY

The blurb of the Rex Collins edition of Wole Soyinka's *Opera Wonyosi* describes the play as a "Nigerian version of Brecht's *Threepenny Opera*, itself a version of Gay's *The Beggar's Opera*." [2] First produced for the University of Ife (now Obafemi Awolowo University) convocation held on December 16, 1977, the play represents a searing indictment of the entire spectrum of the Nigerian society.

Soyinka had been detained for twenty-seven months beginning from July 1967 because of his opposing stance on the Nigerian civil war. Following what he perceived as a continuing threat to his life, he had had to go into self exile in March 1971. On his return after General Yakubu Gowon, the military ruler who originally detained him, had been overthrown in a July 1975 coup, Soyinka met a country that had become deeply mired in corruption, and which, in short, had lost all sense of direction. His response to this development was a series of satirical works. [3] *Opera Wonyosi*, described by Yemi Ogunbiyi as "Soyinka's fifteenth major published play", [4] and which also represents the dramatist's first major production following his assumption of the headship of the Department of Dramatic Arts of the University, stands out as the best known in the series. This chapter

---

1 An earlier version of this chapter was first published in *John Gay's The Beggar's Opera: Adaptations and Re-Writings*. Eds. Uwe Boeker, Ines Detmers & Anna – Christina Giovanopoulos (Amsterdam/New York: Rodopi, 2006): 243 – 271

2 See the blurb of the Rex Collins' edition of the play: Wole Soyinka, *Opera Wonyosi*. London: Rex Collins 1981. The version used in this essay, however, is the one included in *Wole Soyinka: Six Plays*. London: Methuen, 1992. pp. 295 – 407. All further references will be to this latter edition.

3 James Gibbs lists the works at the beginning of chapter eight of his study *Wole Soyinka*. London: Macmillan 1986, p. 128. Those listed include *Before the Blow-out* (1978), *Rice Unlimited* (1981), *Die Still Rev. Dr Godspeak!* (1982) a radio play which later transforms to *Requiem for a Futurologist* (1983), and *Priority Projects*.

4 Yemi Ogunbiyi, "*Opera Wonyosi*: A Study of Soyinka's *Opera Wonyosi*", *Nigeria Magazine*, Nos 128 – 129, 1979, pp. 3 – 14, here 3.

investigates the play as an example of how an appropriate European model can be adapted to address a specific socio-historical situation in the context of post-colonial Africa. The play will be analyzed against the background of John Gay's *The Beggar's Opera* [5] and Bertolt Brecht's *Threepenny Opera*, the two preceding models. [6]

## II. AFRICAN ADAPTATIONS OF EUROPEAN PLAYS

In general, dramatic adaptations have a long history. [7] In European tradition, and as Michael Etherton contends in *The Development of African Drama*, it is part of the process through which "play-texts have survived the process of history." [8] In the specific case of Africa, it is illustrative of the complex relationships existing between the peoples of the continent and the West. The list of African adaptations is fairly long and it includes Ola Rotimi's *The Gods are not to Blame* (re-worked from Sophocles' *King Oedipus*), Athol Fugard's *The Island* (based on Sophocles' *Antigone*), Femi Osofisan's *Tegonni: an African Antigone* (again based on Sophocles' *Antigone*), Wole Soyinka's *The Bacchae of Euripedes* (based on Euripedes's *The Bacchae*), Obotunde Ijimere's *Everyman* (based on the medieval Europe's *Everyman* as specifically adapted in German by Hugo von Hofmannsthal), Femi Osofisan's *Who is Afraid of Solarin* (based on Nikolai Gogol's *The Inspector)*, Zulu Sofola's *The Wizard of Law* (based on the French farcical comedy, *Pierre Pathelin*), Efua Sutherland's *Edufa* (based on Euripedes *Alkestis*), Julius Nyerere's Swahili version of Shakespeare's *Julius Caesar* and, of course, the text under study, Soyinka's *Opera Wonyosi.* [9]

The list is not an exhaustive one. Rather, it represents the best known, and in my view, the more successful of African adaptations of European play-texts. [10] As Etherton further suggests, re-working a play may involve simple superficial change of details such as altering titles, names of characters and the physical set-

---

5 The version used in this essay is the Dover edition of 1973. See John Gay, *The Beggar's Opera*. New York: Dover Publications, 1973

6 The version used here is the Eyre Methuen edition of 1979. See Bertolt Brecht, *The Threepenny Opera*. London: Eyre Methuen, 1979.

7 For recent research on adaptations and re-writings, cf. Martin Middeke and Werner Huber, ed., *Biofictions: The Rewriting of Romantic Lives in Contemporary Fiction and Drama*, Rochester, NY: Camden House 1999;

8 Michael Etherton, *The Development of African Drama*. London: Hutchinson University Library of Africa. 1982, p. 102.

9 For re-writings of Greek tragedies, cf. also Broich, Ulrich, "Post-Colonial Drama and Greek Tragedy". In: Uwe Böker and Hans Sauer (eds.). *Anglistentag 1996 Dresden. Proceedings*. Trier: WVT 1997, 169 – 175.

10 Etherton mentions also a Nigeria Pidgin version of Bertolt Brecht's *The Good Woman of Setzuan* (Etherton, *Development of African Drama*, 104).

ting of the action of the original text. On the other hand, it may entail complete re-working or radical re-casting of the original text. "At one extreme," says Etherton, "this is nothing more than translation; at the other extreme it is a new play: an original play influenced by, or alluding to, an earlier work". [11]

Interestingly, a play that serves to exemplify the first extreme, more or less, is also, arguably, the most popular of all of African adaptations and, undeniably, one of the most successful, frequently staged and widely read texts in contemporary African drama. Rotimi's *The Gods are not to Blame* [12] which re-works Sophocles' *King Oedipus* was first performed in 1968 at the Ori Olokun Cultural Centre, Ile-Ife, Nigeria, under the direction of the playwright himself. Sophocles' original is clearly one of the greatest tragic plays in world theatre history. First performed at about 5th century BC, *King Oedipus* represents one of the few surviving texts of ancient Greek drama and is often included as the first of Sophocles' three plays often published together under the title *The Theban Plays.* [13] Born to Laius, the king of Thebes, Oedipus, the central character in the play, has been fated to kill his father and marry his mother. In an attempt to avert this terrible prediction while at the same time avoiding parricide, the parents ask that the child be cast away in the bush, his feet pierced together. The child however is rescued by a shepherd, handing him over to the king of Corinth who consequently brings him up. Having grown up, Oedipus somehow gets to learn of his fate, and mistaking his foster parents for his real father and mother, he runs away, the aim being to avert the prediction. On his way, Oedipus kills a man who turns out to be King Laius, his true father. He arrives in Thebes and having helped solved the riddle of the sphinx that has hitherto laid siege on the city, is rewarded with the still vacant throne. He marries Jocasta, wife of the former king and incidentally his own true mother.

By the time the play opens, all the above has taken place but the true identity of Oedipus remains unknown. Thus it happens that the action of the play, which depends mainly on irony, consists principally in the unraveling of this identity. A plague actually has befallen the land, and in an attempt to determine the cause, it is revealed that the person who committed the heinous crime of killing the former king still resides within Thebes. In a single-minded pursuit of the villain therefore, Oedipus arrives at himself. He inflicts the punishment he has earlier prescribed for whoever turns out to be responsible for the crime by gouging out his own eyes, and, in addition, abdicating the throne.

Rotimi's *The Gods are not to Blame* follows this story line almost to the letter, re-naming only characters and places: Thebes becomes Kutuje; Corinth, Ijekun-Yemoja; Oedipus, Odewale; Laius, Adetusa; Jocasta, Queen Ojuola; Apollo,

---

[11] Etherton, 103.

[12] Ola Rotimi, The *Gods are not to Blame. London*: Oxford University Press, 1971

[13] Sophocles, *The Theban Plays*. Harmondsworth: Penguin 1981.

Ogun, the Yoruba god of iron; Chorus of Theban elders, townspeople, etc. Directly, a child is born to King Adetusa and Queen Ojuola. It is predicted that he will kill his father and marry his mother, and is therefore asked to be abandoned in the bush. The child is rescued by Alaka, servant to Ogundele, king of Ijekun-Yemoja who gave him to his master to be brought up by Mobike, the queen. Odewale grows up in Ijekun-Yemoja, learns of his fate and thinking Mobike and Ogundele to be his true parents leaves home. He gets involved in a violent quarrel on the way in which he ends up killing his opponent who, as is to turn out, is his true father. He wanders into the land of Kutuje and leads the people in a battle against a neighbouring community, which hitherto has constituted a menace to the people. Victorious, he is rewarded with the throne.

As can be seen, the story remains the same, essentially. Rotimi runs into troubled waters, however, when it comes to transposing the concept of fate into Yoruba sub-soil. Among these people who reside in the South Western part of Nigeria, the gods are neither vengeful, nor is human fate determined unilaterally by them. And when they themselves commit errors, the gods that is, they are made to pay reparations [14]. Indeed, in Yoruba cosmology, before embarking on a journey to the world of the living, every freshly created being approaches Olodumare, the supreme God to determine for him/herself his/her destiny in the world of the living. And even when it so happens that an individual during this process elects something terrible, it can still be averted after birth through appropriate rites of propitiation.

But Rotimi is determined to get round this. What he eventually does is to make Odewale, the central character, at the moment of knowledge deliberately excuse the gods, heaping the blame of his fall on himself and citing hot temper as the cause. But as critics have pointed out, this interpretation, which itself is Aristotelian, remains completely unconvincing and the title of the play stands as nothing but an apology. [15]

Soyinka's *Opera Wonyosi* does not exactly represent the other radical extreme

[14] Soyinka treats this issue of the relationship between the Yorubas and their gods in "Drama and the African World – view," chapter two of his book of essays, *Myth, Literature and the African World*. See Wole Soyinka, *Myth, Literature and the African World* Cambridge: Cambridge University Press, 1976

[15] There are several other problems which Rotimi could not tackle in his adaptation, including the fact that kingship among Yoruba people is hereditary and is neither awarded to a stranger nor, for that matter, a warrior. Also, as a matter of necessity, every traditional Yoruba society consults the oracle to determine what the reign of a candidate for the kingship throne portends before, eventually, taking a decision. For further criticism of *The Gods are not to Blame*, see Robert Plant Armstrong, "Tragedy – Greek and Yoruba: A Cross – Cultural Perspective." *Research in African Literature*, 7 (1976), pp. 23–43; and Akanji Nasiru. "Ola Rotimi's Search for Technique," in *Introduction to West African Literature* (ed.) Kolawole Ogungbesan. Ibadan: Ibadan University Press, 1979 pp. 62–73

indicated in Etherton's paradigm [16]. In fact, taken on the surface, and given the fact that Soyinka remains faithful, up to a point, to the story – line of especially Bertolt Brecht's version, and also because he even retains the original names of some of the characters, *Opera Wonyosi* may be taken as another superficial response to the concept of adaptation. This however will be far from accurate. It seems to me, actually, an evidence of Soyinka's genius that even as he adopts the structure of *Threepenny Opera* in his adaptation, and, as well, retains what Bernth Lindfors has described in "Begging Questions in Wole Soyinka's *Opera Wonyosi*" [17] as a "Gayish agility of wit," he still manages to imbue the dramatic work with a distinctively African – nay Nigerian – character. My approach in this paper then is to place the text side by side the two earlier versions, identifying points of similarity as well as Soyinka's areas of departure and originality. More importantly however, I also intend to locate the play within the Nigerian postcolonial context and, as well, place it within the context of Soyinka's dramatic oeuvre.

In awarding the Nobel prize to him in 1986, the Nobel Academy had, in a citation, described Wole Soyinka as a writer who, "in a wide cultural perspective, fashions the drama of existence". [18] There is no doubt that, as a dramatist, Wole Soyinka's sources are wide and disparate. Simultaneously however, his works are also known to be deeply rooted in his indigenous Yoruba heritage. In *Myth, Literature and the African World*, a book which Soyinka devotes to the elicitation of an African theory of tragedy, the playwright points it out that to the extent that wo/man exists in "a comprehensive world of myth, history and mores," the African world indeed, can be described as unique. The foremost dramatist is quick to add however that this uniqueness is never absolute, that African world indeed "possesses, in common with other cultures, the virtues of complementarity". [19] It seems then that the "wide cultural perspective" which the Nobel citation refers to is in reference to the simultaneous influence on the Nigerian playwright of his indigenous heritage as well as the Hellenic, European and the American avant-garde dramatic practices. The Hellenic impact is more evident in Soyinka's perspective of tragedy, a perspective which, as has been said, receives sustained articulation

---

16 In African Drama, this award should actually go to Athol Fugard, John Kani and Winston Ntshona's appropriation of Sophocle's *Antigone* in their play *The Island*. See Athol Fugard, *Statements: Three Plays*. London: Oxford University Press, 1974.

17 Actually, this essay by Lindfors has done a good job of identifying the details of Soyinka's debt to both John Gay and Bertolt Brecht. See Bernth Lindfors, "Begging Questions in Wole Soyinka's Opera Wonyosi," in *Research on Wole Soyinka* ed. James Gibbs & Bernth Lindfors, Trenton, NJ: Africa World Press, 1993: pp149 – 159

18 Cited from Biodun Jeyifo, *Wole Soyinka: A Voice from Africa*. New York. IMG Educators 1990, 2.

19 Wole Soyinka, *Myth, Literature and the African World*, Cambridge: Cambridge University Press, 1976. xii n

in *Myth, Literature and the African World*, his first book of essays, and which has also been well illustrated in his important tragic works, including *Death and the King's Horseman* (1975), *The Strong Breed* (1964), *The Road* (1965) *Madmen and Specialists* (1970) and *The Bacchae of Euripedes* (1973).

Soyinka's theory of tragedy is rooted in the myth of origin of the Yorubas, Soyinka's original group. [20] In the beginning, according to the myth, there existed only Orisa Nla, the supreme godhead, who embodied within himself, the mortal and immortal essences. Orisa Nla had a slave, Atunda, (meaning, literally, recreation) who attended to him. One day, as Orisa Nla tended his farm at the foot of the hill, Atunda rebelled, smashing a huge boulder on his master, causing him to roll down the abyss, broken into a thousand and one fragments. Each of these fragments then transformed into a being, with the mortal shards becoming human beings and the immortal ones the gods, and while the former took over the earth, the latter established themselves in heaven. But the anguish of separation was great for both sides since, as has been stated, they were originally of the same essences. Both continued to be tormented by a feeling of incompleteness until the gods felt that they had had enough, deciding there and then to undertake a pilgrimage to earth. On setting out, however, they were to discover that a thick, immense and chaotic outgrowth had sealed off the abyss of transition, making passage completely impossible. One by one, the gods tried but could not cut through the growth. One by one, they despaired. Until Ogun, the god of iron and of war surged forward, plunging into the abyss, summoning others to follow, mobilizing raw, elemental will, and cutting a path through the gulf, linking heaven with earth.

In *Myth, Literature and the African World*, Soyinka describes the god, Ogun, as "a combination of Dionysian, Apollonian and Promethean principles". [21] He is the god of iron and of war, but also the god of creativity and of destructiveness. He watches over the road, is the patron of hunters and also of artists. Quoting from his praise – chants in the same book, Soyinka describes him as the "refuge of the down-trodden," one who in order to "rescue slaves, unleashed the judgement of war" and who "stands bulwark to offsprings of the dead of heaven". [22] Dionysos

[20] For more on this myth as well as Soyinka's employment of same, see *Ulli Beier, Orisa Liberates the Mind: Wole Soyinka in Conversation with Ulli Beier on Yoruba Religion*. Bayreuth: Iwalewa Haus, 1992; Abiola Irele, "Tradition and the Yoruba Writer: D.O. Fagunwa, Amos Tutuola and Wole Soyinka," in *The African Experience in Literature and Ideology*. Bloomington IN: Indiana University Press, 1990 pp. 174 – 197; Stephan Larsen, *A Writer and his Gods: A Study of the Importance of Myths and Religious Ideas to the Writings of Wole Soyinka*. Stockholm: University of Stockholm Department of the History of Literature, 1993; and Oyin Ogunba, "Traditional African Festival Drama," in Oyin Ogunba & Abiola Irele (eds.) *Theatre in Africa*. Ibadan: Ibadan University Press, 1978: pp. 3 – 26

[21] Soyinka, *Myth, Literature and the African World*, 26.

[22] Ibid., 26 – 27.

is the Greek god of wine and of revelry. Ogun is also a lover of wine and women. His staff of worship bears close resemblance to the *thyrsus* of Dionysos while his sacrificial dog, dismembered "limb from limb" brings into consciousness the fate suffered by Zagreus, son of Zeus. Then, since Ogun's act of hubris was carried out on behalf of the community, he can also be seen as a partner to Prometheus, the Greek god who stole fire from heaven, bringing it down for the use of humanity. In Yoruba metaphysical worldview, Ogun is the first actor, and his act represents the first tragic act. For communal goodness, he dared the dark void of transition and, but for his enormous will, would have been rendered asunder by cosmic wind. The Yorubas believe in three levels of existence – the worlds of the dead/gods, the living and, the unborn – and the constant interaction between the different realms. The passage linking them is what Soyinka has described in what perhaps remains his best-known essay as "the fourth stage."[23] To sustain harmony in the cosmos, it is this fourth stage, the gulf of transition, that must be constantly kept open, constantly diminished with offerings and sacrifices. In African ritual tragedy then, the tragic protagonist is the one who surrenders his individuation, undertaking a journey through the primal abyss in order to commune with the gods and the ancestors. Ogun was the first being to undertake such a task, and his example serves as the primary motivating factor for the tragic hero. Soyinka remarks:

> The actor in ritual drama operates in the same way (as Ogun did on the first day). He prepares mentally and physically for his disintegration and re-assembly within the universal womb of origin, experiences the transitional yet inchoate matrix of death and being. Such an actor in the role of the protagonist becomes the unresisting mouthpiece of the god, uttering sounds which he barely comprehends but which are reflections of the awesome glimpse of that transitional gulf, the seething cauldron of the dark world – will and psyche. Tragic feeling in Yoruba drama stems from sympathetic knowledge of the protagonist's foray into this psychic abyss of re-creative energies.[24]

The foregoing discussion is useful for understanding Soyinka's tragic works. In all the major tragedies penned so far by the Nobel laureate, there is always a tragic issue, often of profound concern for the community. There is a protagonist hero, also always an individual of great will, who for the sake of communal well-being demonstrates a readiness to wade through the gulf of transition. Eman in *The Strong Breed*[25] is for example born into the family of ritual careers. Unready to take on the responsibility bestowed on him by his inheritance, he flees his land of

---

[23] "The Fourth Stage," written much earlier than the other four essays in *Myth, Literature and the African World* is included in the book as an appendix. See *Myth, Literature and the African World*, pp. 140 – 160

[24] *Myth, Literature and the African World*, p. 30

[25] Wole Soyinka, *The Strong Breed* in *Wole Soyinka: Collected Plays I.* Oxford: Oxford University Press, pp. 113 – 146

birth. Once in a season of ritual cleansing in his land of exile however, Eman finds himself stepping forward as that year's scapegoat. Overtaken by his blood, Eman lays down his life on behalf of that particular community.

But perhaps the most profound dramatic demonstration, so far, of this issue in Soyinka's oeuvre of tragedy is *Death and the King's Horseman* [26]. The play is in fact based on an actual incident, which occurred in the ancient Yoruba town of Oyo in 1946. Alaafin Ladigbolu, the monarch of the ancient town had just passed on. As has been made clear, death in most African traditions is not a cessation of life but a transition to another realm of existence, the world of the ancestors and also of the gods. Consequently it is part of the belief that in order to maintain a harmonious relationship with this other world, the living must properly send off the dead. For the king that had just transited to the world of the ancestors therefore, part of the funeral rites entails the ritual suicide on the night of the final ceremonies, of Olokun Esin the king's chief horseman. The title, Olokun Esin was an important one in Oyo. The holder of the position maintained very close relationship with any reigning Alaafin, enjoying privileges that could only be surpassed by those of the king. This derives from the people's appreciation of the nature of the responsibility that he carries on their behalf. It was the duty of the head of the king's stable to surrender his individuation on the night his master was to be buried and take a plunge on behalf of his community through the abyss of transition in order to maintain close companionship with the dead king in the world beyond. This, indeed, was what any Elesin lived for. But as it happened in 1946, following the death of Alafin Ladigbolu, the then commander of the stable failed to carry out his role, seeking refuge instead with Pilkings, the colonial district officer who had by then effectively hijacked ultimate authority/power from the traditional ruler.

In adapting this historical material in *Death and the King's Horseman*, Soyinka fixes the action of the play on the very night Elesin Oba is expected to commit suicide. The play opens as the chief character engages in a final ritual dance round the market. The atmosphere is charged naturally. But in spite of this, and as Tejumola Olaniyan has observed in *Scars of Conquest/Masks of Resistance* [27], it is clear from his actions and behaviour that Elesin is not at all ready for the gargantuan task expected of him. To everybody's surprise, he even decides to take on a new bride on this most important night of his life. As he wavers and wanders, Simon Pilkings, the white district officer intervenes and effects his arrest. Olunde, Elesin's first son, a medical student in England who has travelled down to perform his father's funeral feels unable to swallow the dishonourable

[26] Wole Soyinka, *Death and the King's Horseman* in *Soyinka: Six Plays*, 143–220

[27] Tejumola Olaniyan, *Scars of Conquest, Masks of Resistance: The Invention of Cultural Identity in African, African American and Caribbean Drama*. New York: Oxford University Press, 1995.

reputation this entails for the family. In a great, determined effort to preserve the family's integrity, he summons his will and commits suicide in place of his father. Confronted later with his son's dead body, Elesin also strangles himself. Here is the man's praise-singer as he drives home the implication of the incident for the history of the race:

> Elesin Oba, we placed the reins of the world in your hands yet you watched it plunge over the edge of the bitter precipice. You sat with folded arms while evil strangers tilted the world from its course and crashed it beyond the edge of emptiness – you muttered there is little that one man can do, you left us floundering in a blind future. Your heir has taken the burden on himself. What the end will be, we are not gods to tell. [28]

Even though he finally commits suicide, Elesin can no longer be considered as the Ogunnian character in the play. Having dilly-dallied, he loses that privileged position to Olunde, his son. And in the preface to the play, Soyinka warns both the reader and the would-be producer against investing too much energy in the political interpretation. "The Colonial Factor is an incident, a catalytic incident merely", he says in the said prefatory note. "The confrontation in the play," he continues, "is largely metaphysical, contained in the human vehicle which is Elesin and the universe of the Yoruba mind-the world of the living, the dead and the unborn, and the numinous passage which links all: transition". [29] Of course, there is no way any reader can miss the cultural interpretation in the play, and, indeed, the work has often been read as an affirmation of the Yoruba metaphysical worldview. In addition, and as a further effort at ensuring that this particular perspective is upheld, the playwright also makes great effort to see to it that the blame for Elesin's failure is put squarely at the man's doorstep. The society holds Elesin up as a redeemer and the man has lived his whole life in expectation of the appointed moment. Yet, when the decisive hour arrives, there is nothing to indicate that he is ready for this enormous responsibility. Elesin is found in the market place, dancing among the women. He even decides to take a new bride at this very last moment of his life, an act that further assaults his already weak resolve. Elesin wavers in the performance of his communal task and it is this that presents Pilkings the opportunity to intervene.

But as important as the metaphysical interpretation is, there is no way to underplay the aspects of the historical confrontation in the play. Soyinka himself confesses to having set the action of the play back by two years in order to make it coincide with the period of the Second World War. And this, as he states, is for "minor reasons of dramaturgy". [30] It is for this same "minor reasons," presumably,

---

28 *Death and the King's Horseman* in *Wole Soyinka: Six Plays*, p. 218

29 Ibid. 145

30 Ibid. 145

that Elesin's first son transforms from Muraina, a trader that he was in Ghana in actual history to Olunde, a medical student in England. Pilkings' action in assisting the boy to secure admission in England is in order to make him (Olunde) escape what he – Pilkings – sees as a pagan tradition. However, the young man returns after four years at his study to take on his father's role. Olunde's suicide indeed makes nonsense of his colonial education. His exposure in England also makes it possible for him to be able to underline the contradictions in European civilization and this he articulates very cogently in his discursive encounter with the Pilkings: "[...] I had plenty of time to study your people", Olunde says to Jane, Pilkings' wife, in a statement that sums up his position on western culture, "I saw nothing, finally, that gave you the right to pass judgment on other peoples and their ways. Nothing at all". [31]

## III. SOYINKA THE SATIRIST

Soyinka indeed is an extremely versatile playwright. He has equal reputation both as a tragedian and as a satirist. He has, indeed, through the latter medium continued to expose the different ills of his contemporary Nigerian society in particular, and the African continent in general.

Here, and again as in his tragic works, the dramatist has been both original and eclectic. Of course, his perspective of this medium has been honed since as far back as the early sixties. The perspective finds its first articulation in a little known essay titled "The Lysistrata of Aristophanes" now published in *Art, Dialogue and Outrage*, a collection of Soyinka's essays edited by Biodun Jeyifo. [32] In this essay, and as its title suggests, Soyinka studies *Lysistrata*, the satiric play by Aristophanes, the well known comedian of ancient Greece.

Soyinka first of all remarks that satire often exaggerates to a ludicrous degree. Because of this, as he further points out, it generates laughter, which laughter issues as much from an attitude of superiority on the part of the audience as it does also from anxiety and fear. The foremost dramatist actually opens the essay by pointing out directly that it is the sinister aspect of satire which provokes this fear. And this aspect inheres in the thoughts that the genre often provokes: that of the possibility that what is being presented on stage might just happen.

Soyinka pointedly approves in his paper the way, at least in his opinion, Aristophanes' *Lysistrata* "teeters successfully on this knife-edge of laughter-superiority and self-centered fear". [33] Towards the end he adds that beside the

---

31 Ibid. 196

32 Wole Soyinka, "The Lysistrata of Aristophanes". In: *Art, Dialogue and Outrage: Essays on African Literature and Culture*. Ibadan: New Horn 1988, 35 – 41.

33 Ibid., 35.

tendency to analyze, denounce, and distort the identified ills of his society, Aristophanes also possesses an additional principle as a dramatist:

> Aristophanes [ ... ] reveals more than the satirical dramatist's basic iconoclasm. A passion for certain humane values pervades his work and I believe that in that phrase, 'Till they discover humanity's meaning' may be found his most clearly stated sense of mission, the impulse behind his irreverence, his gaily uncompromising stance against intellectual cant, hypocrisy and cruelty.[34]

In exploring Soyinka's satiric oeuvre, there is no way to doubt that he has been guided, at least in part, by the perspective that he has expressed in this essay. In play after play, Soyinka has continued to explore the different negative principles plaguing contemporary African societies. It is the Nigerian dramatist's express belief that such "turning up of the maggot-infested underside of the compost heap" (*OW*, foreword) of society must of necessity continue till humanity discovers its meaning.

Two major pre-occupations are discernible in Wole Soyinka's satiric works. The first, broadly, can be described as religious charlatanism and the second, socio-political decadence. Exploring the former theme are such works as *The Trials of Brother Jero* (1964), *Jero's Metamorphosis* (1973) and *Requiem for a Futurologist* (1985). Of the three, the last, which also is the most recent, appears to be the most ludicrous and equally the most daring. There existed in Nigeria in the late seventies and early eighties a lot of parapsychologists and so-called prophets who claimed to be able to predict the future. A particularly notorious one among them was Dr. Godspower Oyewole whose predictions were taken very seriously and were actually believed by several people. *Requiem for a Futurologist* exposes these charlatans to ridicule while also deriding the people for their levels of gullibility and follies. The play presents two rival futurologists, namely Dr. Godspower Igbehodan and Brother Eleazar Hosannah. In his desperate bid to supplant the former who actually is his boss, the latter not only predicts Igbehodan's death, he also follows it up quickly by announcing his obituary.[35] In their gullibility, the people not only take this to be true, but also troop out in large number to catch a glimpse of the corpse of Dr. Igbehodan. We are confronted with this man pleading desperately before the huge gathering that he is not dead but without anybody ready to believe him. As the action of the play moves toward the end, Igbehodan makes a desperate attempt to turn the table against Eleazar by announcing that the latter had also been knocked down by a lorry. As this fails to moves the crowd, he tries the practical option of hacking down his assailant. Eventually, he is prevailed upon by Dr. Semuwe, a fake psychiatrist – in actuality,

34 Ibid., 40.

35 Jonathan Swift did already the same with his predictions of [see text at the end of your essay].

Brother Hossana in disguise – to lie down still as if he is dead. It was at this point that Eleazar Hossana steps in, bowing in acknowledgment as he is hailed by the people as Nostradamus.

## IV. Opera Wonyosi as a Satire

Soyinka's works of socio-political satire include *Opera Wonyosi*, *A Play of Giants* (1984), *From Zia with Love* (1992), *A Scourge of Hyacinth* (1992) and *The Beatification of Area Boys* (1995). The playwright himself calls *Opera Wonyosi* in the foreword to the London edition "an exposition of levels of power in practice" [36]. It is a very biting play. It is as much a savage attack on the leadership of the Nigerian society as it is on the citizenry. However, because it was first staged for an official ceremony of a University, its audience comprised top government functionaries including even the then military governor of Oyo state, Brigadier David Jemibewon. The sharp criticism not withstanding, the functionaries watched the play till the very end. Their reaction was known later when the plan to take the production to the seat of government in Lagos was suddenly cancelled. Commenting on this development, James Gibbs argues that it was "the proof of the power of Soyinka's production", which makes the play to be "confined to Ife". [37]

With a full-blown orchestra and well over fifty actors and actresses, *Opera Wonyosi* represents an extremely demanding production. In producing it in 1977, however, Soyinka had a lot going for him. In the first place, and as the Head of the Department of Dramatic Arts, the playwright producer had full control of the entire manpower – students and staff – of his Department. Secondly, as the chairman of the management committee of the then newly commissioned Oduduwa Hall, he also had no problem securing the use of a well-equipped theatre. Thirdly, since the play itself was commissioned for an official function of the University – the convocation, that is – it was clear that Soyinka had relatively generous funding for its staging.

## V. Gay's The Beggar's Opera

The production of *The Beggars' Opera*, John Gay's original, did not however meet with the same kind of luck in 1728. In fact, Gay had problems getting the play accepted for production. It was flatly turned down by Drury Lane, one of the leading theatre companies in London at the time for, according to Calhoun Winton, the play's "out-of-the-way, experimental, and non-standard" nature. [38] It was

[36] *Opera Wonyosi* in *Soyinka: Six Plays*, p. 298

[37] Gibbs, *Soyinka*, 135.

[38] Calhoun Winton, *John Gay and the London Theatre*. Kentucky: The University Press of Kentucky 1993, 96.

with great reluctance that Lincoln Inn, a company which then was experiencing a slow-down took it up. Even so, the entire period of rehearsal was characterized by intense anxieties. "Right down to opening night", as Winton writes, "there was every reason for Rich and his company to have second thoughts about presenting a new production". [39] Drury Lane's *The Provoked Husband* was demolishing competition. The premiere of John Sturmy's *Sesostris* grossed only sixty pounds on opening night (17 January) at Lincoln's Inn, dragged on for second author's benefit of forty-seven pounds on the 23rd and closed forever on the 27th of January 1728. *The Beggar's Opera* was next up. It was not a promising atmosphere for Gay's new play.

It was thus with great apprehension that the play opened on Monday January 29, 1728. By Thursday February 1 however, newspapers had already started commenting positively on the production, and by February 3, it had become very clear that the play represented a huge commercial success. According to Winton, "the re-education campaign of the opposition, the programme of finding and pointing out specific political propaganda, did not begin until *The Beggar's Opera* was securely established as a hit". [40]

The question is: where lies the propaganda in the play? John Gay was said to have expected an improvement in his material situation following the death of George I in June 1727 and the consequent coming into office of the Prince of Wales as George II. The King, however, chose to retain Robert Walpole in power and all that Gay received by way of offer was "nothing more alluring than the post of 'gentleman usher' to the Princess Louisa at a salary of about 200 pound a year". [41] Rejecting the offer, Gay was thus supposed to have set upon writing *The Beggar's Opera* in frustration. Thus, it was speculated that Macheath, the common criminal in the play stood for Robert Walpole.

## VI. Brecht's Threepenny Opera

Coming in 1928, two hundred years after Gay's debut, Bertolt Brecht's adaptation follows the basic outline of the original. As was the case with John Gay's play, *The Threepenny Opera* also represents the work that established a reputation for Brecht as a playwright. The work has been produced several times over and has been translated into several European languages as well as adapted into film, novel and music. Though set in London, *The Threepenny Opera* is well known as a criticism of the bourgeois inclinations of the defunct Weimar's Republic. The play

---

39 *John Gay and the London Theatre*, 97

40 Ibid., 99.

41 Oswald Doughty, "Introduction" in John Gay, *The Beggar's Opera*. New York: Dover Publications, 1973 p. x

indeed is full of open ideological statements. Pertinent examples in this regard are the first and second finale songs which, respectively, focus on the "insecurity of the human condition" and "what keeps mankind alive". And in the third finale where, a reprieve having been announced for Macheath, the man who has just been rescued from the gallows himself proclaims joyously before the spectators that "When you're most despairing/The clouds may be clearing". [42]

But beside this, there are several innovations in *The Threepenny Opera*. The most obvious of these perhaps are the dialogues which had to be completely re-written, and the songs which were freshly composed and set to music by Kurt Weill. Brecht also sets his own version against an impending coronation of the queen. Innovations in the area of characterization include the distinguished areas of specialization drawn for each of Peachum and Macheath. While the latter still remains the kingpin of criminals, the former is now characterized as the proprietor of the Beggar's Friend Limited, one who makes up people as beggars and sends them out to the streets to beg. Brown, the high Sheriff of London, is almost completely different from Lockit, John Gay's character from whom he was originally created. Brown is a more sinister person, collaborating at the same time with both Peachum and Macheath. He is actually supposed to be a close friend of the latter, one together with whom he served as a soldier in India. But while cutting corners with Macheath, he is also involved in deals with Peachum. Brecht also plays out in act one, scene two, the marriage between Macheath and Polly which takes place in a stable, attended both by Reverend Kimball – another creation of Brecht – and Tiger Brown himself. The scene affords the audience the opportunity to meet the members of Macheath's gang and to have first hand information as regards their deadliness. All the materials used for the wedding were stolen and some of the unfortunate owners of the property have either been inflicted with serious wounds or have been completely eliminated.

There are a number of other innovations worked by Brecht into his own adaptation, above all the ending. As has been pointed out, *The Beggar's Opera*, among other things, is supposed to be a criticism of Handel's opera, and it actually enjoys the reputation of being the play that renders the Italian opera unpopular in England. [43] At the end of the play, Gay simply invites both Player and Beggar, the two characters who open the play, back to the stage. "But, honest Friend, I hope you don't intend that Macheath shall be really executed", so goes the comment Player directs at Beggar as soon as the two have entered the stage:

*Beggar*: Most certainly, Sir. – To make the Piece perfect, I was for doing strict poetical Justice – Macheath is to be hang'd; or transported.

---

42 The *Threepenny Opera*, 79

43 For a discussion of this aspect, see Böker in this volume.

*Player*: Why then, Friend, this is a downright deep tragedy. The Catastrophe is manifestly wrong, for an Opera must end happily.

*Beggar*: Your objection, Sir, is very just, and is easily remov'd. For you must allow, that in this kind of Drama, 'tis no matter how absurdly things are brought about – So – you Rabble there – run and cry, A Reprieve! – let the prisoner be brought back to his Wives in Triumph. (*BO* 92)

This is how Macheath is set free in order to, as Player puts it again, "comply with the Taste of the Town." And the play ends with a celebration.

Since there was no Italian opera to travestize in 1928, Brecht has to achieve a similar ending through another means. In *The Threepenny Opera*, it is Peachum, the man who sets Macheath up in the first instance who also rescues him from the hangman's noose. According to the stage instruction, Macheath is already standing on top of the gallows' steps when Peachum comes out to speak:

Dear audience, we now are coming to
The point where we must hang him by the neck
Because it is the Christian thing to do
Proving that men must pay for what they take.

But as we want to keep our fingers clean
And you're the people we can't risk offending
We thought we'd better do without this scene
And substitute instead a different ending.

Since this is opera, not life, you'll see
Justice give way before humanity.
So now, to stop our story in its course
Enter the royal official on his horse. (*Threepenny Opera,* 78)

With this, Brown comes in on horseback to announce the release of Macheath. The order is supposed to be from the queen and the reason for it is her coronation. "So it all turned out nicely in the end", thus says Mrs. Peachum. And both herself and her husband join to point out that things do not always work out this way in real life, that *deus ex machina* does not happen too often in actuality.

## VII. SOYINKA'S CRITICISM OF THE NIGERIAN SOCIETY

*Opera Wonyosi* projects the grimmest ending of the three versions. There is a reprieve for Macheath of course but this is against the situation of a firm continuation of the frightening evils of the present. The context was a real life event, and it was the coronation of Jean Bedel Bokassa, the then military dictator of Central

African Republic as Emperor for life. Actually, Macheath here is to be killed by firing squad, in the typical fashion of public executions of armed robbers in Nigeria. He has already been wheeled to the spot and the soldiers have taken positions. Macheath makes his last speech and Officer prepares to shout the order to shoot when a special courier arrives to announce a "general Amnesty for all common criminals." There is an elaborate warning that "this great condescension shall not, repeat shall not, extend to anyone accused or convicted of crimes of a political nature" [44]. In the midst of the jubilation that follows, the new emperor himself enters. The last stage instruction reads thus:

> Enter Boky in his Imperial robes, drawn in a chariot by four stalwarts. He drives across, and a procession forms behind him in the following order: The Priests; the Uniformed Services; Chief Anikura and Macheath who first go through a dumb-play of 'After you' courtesies; then fall in step with each other, followed by women; the Gangs; the Whores; the General Rabble. [45]

As far as dramatic conflict goes, and much like the two preceding versions, Polly remains at the centre of *Opera Wonyosi*. Against the wishes of her parents, the young lady gets married to Macheath, the armed robber. As an extremely resourceful person who is determined to protect his business secrets however, Anikura plots Macheath's arrest. The latter is tried and sentenced to death by firing squad. The very moment when hot lead is about to be pumped into his body, the special messenger arrives to deliver the message of salvation.

The thematic details packed by Soyinka into this simple story line is quite dense and multi-dimensional. The play represents indeed a savage attack on corrupt, oppressive power, and also a severe criticism of the general populace. In *Wole Soyinka. Politics, Poetics and Postcolonialism*, Biodun Jeyifo groups the play together with what he describes as outstanding examples of Soyinka's "Power Plays," listing the other members of the corpus as *Kongi's Harvest*, *A Play of Giants* and *From Zia with Love*. Arguing further, Jeyifo states that the question of oppressive power and "reactionary violence," represents a common frame of reference for all these plays, adding though that they do differ, and to use his exact words, "in their underlying conception of dramatic action, theatrical technique, and tone [...]". [46] Focusing specifically now on the play in question, Jeyifo sees the target of Soyinka's attacks as the "Nigerian military dictatorship of the initial

---

[44] *Opera Wonyosi* in *Wole Soyinka: Six Plays*, p. 403

[45] Ibid., 404

[46] Biodun Jeyifo, *Wole Soyinka: Politics, Poetics and Postcolonialism*, (Cambridge: Cambridge University Press, 2004 p. 94

phase of the 'oil boom' years (1973 – 1978), and the 'empire' proclaimed by Jean Bedel Bokasa in the Central African Republic in the same period".[47]

Brian Crow's position is similar to that of Jeyifo. To him, *Opera Wonyosi*, though the earliest of Soyinka's plays dealing with the theme of power, also represents "the most powerful" of the playwright's works focusing on the same subject. Arguing further, Crow contends that even while the play "alludes to a host of abuses and scandals during the Gowon era, [...] its chief target are 'Emperor' Bokassa of Central African Empire and the Nigerian military, in the sinister person of the psychopathic Colonel Moses".[48]

Both critics are right, to be sure, and I have myself noted this point about the play's major pre-occupation earlier on in this essay. What needs to be added at this point is that *Opera Wonyosi*, in addition to its deliberate focus on military dictatorship, is at the same time concerned with a number of salient problems bedevilling Nigeria. This includes the phenomenon of armed robbery, a logical consequence of squandermania and reckless lifestyle of upper and middle class Nigerians in the wake of the oil boom of the seventies. The government of Yakubu Gowon had, at the time, responded to the development unimaginatively by promulgating a decree prescribing death by firing squad for people convicted of the crimes. In no time, the public execution of robbers at the Atlantic waterfront in Lagos soon became a big spectacle, watched by the highly as well as the lowly placed in the society. Soyinka treats this sadistic response with great revulsion in the play.

Anikura's Home from Home for the Homeless is also of very great significance. Through it, Soyinka deals with the question of the destruction of merit and objectivity in Nigerian society. Again, beginning from the early seventies, appointment of people into professional and political positions in Nigeria are made, often less due to the level of competence and quality of minds of the individuals concerned, but rather due to the amount of influence the people are able to muster, the connection they have in high places and the degree of self-debasement they are ready to undergo. In short, to secure any position in contemporary Nigerian society, one has to be ready to massage the ego of the highly-placed, grease their palms and even lick their boots. The effect of the development has been tragic for the Nigerian society. It is one of the major factors responsible of the collapse of the system, and also of the destruction of infrastructural facilities. It is the reason why absolutely nothing works.

This situation comes under harsh satire in *Opera Wonyosi*. In the play, Anikura's home of beggars represents the institution where the political jobbers of the society undergo requisite training in the art of begging. Bamgbapo has al-

---

[47] Ibid., 95)

[48] Brian Crow, "Soyinka and his Radical Critics", in *Perspectives on Wole Soyinka: Freedom and Complexity* (Jackson: University Press of Mississippi, 2001, p. 101

ready begged his way into professorship, and several top positions in government, including the chairmanship of the board of Mining Corporation. Currently however he is in Anikura's begging home, undertaking a refresher course in the art of boot-licking. On graduation, as Anikura himself tells us, Professor Bamgbapo should have no problem bagging the chairmanship of the National Haulage, Air Freight and Shipping Lines. On his own, Alatako, a trained lawyer has his eyes on the position of the Attorney General of the federation. He is also in the same home trying to acquire skills on how to beg his way up to the post within a time-period of three years. "He who begs," as Soyinka puts it in the play, indeed "bags." [49]

The question may now be asked: if, as it is, *Opera Wonyosi* represents a no-hold-barred criticism of the Nigerian society, how come that the physical action of the play is located in another country? How, indeed, does it happen that the coronation of Jean Bedel Bokassa of Central African Republic is made central to the play? Well, the first thing to say to this, perhaps, is that *Opera Wonyosi* is a very ambitious play, one, actually, that projects very, very complex dimensions. As has earlier been stated, the play is also set in the context of military dictatorship in Africa. Beside Bokassa, at least three other hideous dictators held sway in different countries of Africa as at the time *Opera Wonyosi* was being produced for the first time in 1977. They were "President-for Life" Idi Amin Dada of Uganda, Field Marshall Mobutu Sese Seko of Zaire (now Democratic Republic of Congo) and "President for Keeps" Marcias Nguema of Equatorial Guinea. Soyinka obviously considers it important to expose the hideousness and buffoonery of these mutants to savage criticism. The playwright must have singled out Bokassa precisely because, of all of them, he was the one that got his 'parliament' to pass a bill proclaiming him as emperor – for – life, the coronation ceremony of which was to cost his country almost the entire budget for that year. In realizing his two ambitions in the play exposing the decadence of Nigerian society and lampooning the tyrants of Africa – what Soyinka does is to create an expatriate community of Nigerians in Bangui, the capital city of Central African Republic. The explanation that the playwright works out for this situation is that the people had fled down to the country in droves during the Nigerian civil war that lasted between 1967 and 1970 and, having established themselves in Bangui, have decided to stay back even after the war had ended. However, and in spite of their expatriate status, they are also supposed to have imported all the habits currently prevalent at home. What makes this possible is the apparent understanding between the governments of the two countries. Tiger Brown, for example, is supposed to be a security expert who has been on loan to Bokassa right from the pre-war days. It is the same explanation that Soyinka works out for the characters that he has had to create afresh

49 *Opera Wonyosi* in *Wole Soyinka: Six Plays*, 382

by himself. Colonel Moses is projected as a legal and security adviser to Central Africa. Bamgbapo, Professor and Chairman of Nigeria's Mining Corporation, is spending his leave undertaking a refresher course in Chief Anikura's Home from Home for the Homeless while Alatako, whose ambition is to become the Attorney General of the Nigerian Federation has also had to enroll for training in the art of begging in the same begging home. The point that Soyinka thereby makes is that every aspect of the Nigerian society is infected; that every part is rotten and that there is nothing left that could be described as principled, decent or honest. There absolutely is no merit. Everybody begs; and for everything.

It is probably important to, at this point, present a summary of the plot of the play. The play opens with Dee Jay's introductions. Dee Jay, is the master of ceremonies and more should be said about the nature of his role, later. Anyhow, Dee Jay ends this first appearance of his by introducing Chief Anikura, Soyinka's own Peachum, presenting him as "King of Beggars (and) a professional artist who belongs to the school known all through the ages as Con Art" [50] From this point, and although some of the characters, just like Anikura, may bear different names, the story is the same, more or less, as in *Threepenny Opera*. This continues up to the scene of the wedding ceremonies between Macheath and Polly. In the scene after this, Emperor Boky himself appears on stage. What he does is to introduce himself, generally. The spectators are able to see him for who he is: a buffoon, a tyrant and a beast – all rolled into one. One of the methods through which Soyinka is able to achieve this effectively is the historical incident that he brings in. Historically, Bokassa was known to have ordered the mauling down by gunfire of hundreds of school children who had protested against the introduction of a school uniform carrying his picture, the contract of which was handled by his wife. In *Opera Wonyosi*, Commissioner Brown it is who comes in to report the demonstration to Boky. The emperor takes it badly, of course, ordering that the children be brought before him and warning darkly that Brown himself would pay dearly for it should there be any disturbance during the coronation ceremonies. "If there is a disturbance", as he tells Brown, "we would of course expel all your countrymen – without notice, without compensation, and without – you" [51]

Soyinka follows Brecht again from here but is to depart again after Macheath has been arrested. No doubt, his own Macheath is the most sophisticated of the three. He is not just a common criminal, but one with a vast network of connections, what with his business shares in banks as well as several other multinational companies including Igbeti Screwall Investments Limited. [52] Through Polly,

---

[50] *Opera Wonyosi* in *Wole Soyinka: Six Plays*, 303

[51] ibid., 337

[52] Igbeti was a completely obscure town in Western part of Nigeria until the early seventies when lodes of marble deposits were discovered there in abundance. Of course, with scores of com-

Macheath has smartly acquired four thousand shares from Screwall Investments and has given out three-fourth of it as present to Commissioner Brown, Emperor Boky and one or two of his relatives, the Director of Prisons and the Deputy Chief Justice of the Empire. It was this last officer who first signs the stay of execution order and thereafter awards an appeal to Macheath. The rest of the story, of course, is clear.

To get Macheath re-arrested, Anikura blackmails Colonel Moses, the legal and security adviser and the latter agrees to get the Emperor to sign a decree retroactively repealing the Right of Appeal. It has earlier been seen how Macheath secures a final reprieve but it is important to quote, at least in part, Anikura's final speech:

> We men of influence – of power if you like – respect one another. We speak the same language, so we usually work things out. As for you lot, remember, it's not everyday the Emperor's Courier timely arrives, repairing wrongs, sustaining rights, and neatly installing the Back-to-Square-One.[53]

This, no doubt, is a very sad commentary, and is certainly a great departure from Peachum's statement at the end of *The Threepenny Opera*. As pointed out earlier, Brecht's aim in getting his chief character to make the last statement is to subvert any illusion of a one-to-one correspondence between actuality and theatre. Anikura's statement, on the other hand, represents a direct commentary on what goes on in the society. Different rules apply, as he seems to say, between the highly placed people, on the one hand, and the general run of the citizenry on the other. While the former carry out the big robberies, it is the latter who get executed for petty stealing!

*Opera Wonyosi* comments on a vast gamut of issues, all of which could hardly be exhausted in a single essay. One issue that bears mentioning, however, is the episode of unknown victim as played out in scene four. Indeed, in Nigeria of the late seventies and eighties it was common to find human corpses littering the streets; and it stands as a measure of government's indifference that not only were the causes of these deaths – which mostly could be traced to ritual murders, armed robberies and hit-and-run-drivers – left uninvestigated, the bodies were in addition always left to decompose in the open. So prevalent was this incident in the seventies that a social crusader, Dr. Tai Solarin, took it upon himself to pick these bodies, put them in a coffin and thereafter deposit them in front of government's offices. Soyinka seizes on a key moment to comment on this situation in *Opera*

---

panies from different parts of the globe as well as several African Heads of States expressing interest in the resources, it should not be difficult to imagine how this otherwise drab town suddenly began to feature in prime time news.

53 *Opera Wonyosi* in *Wole Soyinka: Six Plays*, 403

*Wonyosi*. Anikura has just succeeded in blackmailing Commissioner Brown into agreeing to get Macheath arrested and as the poor police officer turns to go, the king of beggars drives in a further jab: "There are corpses lying everywhere, you don't busy yourself tracking down their killers, oh no."[54] And to Brown's response which is to the effect that he never sees any corpses, De Madam retorts "I bet you don't. Your friend Macheath always tells you where they are so you can look the other way." Thus ensues the following exchange:

> *De Madam*: … .Take that Doctor…
> *Anikura*: And the lawyer…
> *Beggar*: What of the Musician…
> *Another*: There was that schoolboy…
> *Another*: Even a copper…
> Another: And the pastor…
> Officer: My own sister…
> Officer: Entire family wiped out…
> Officer: The trade unionist
> Anikura: Civil Servants
> De Madam: That Alhaja…
> Beggar: The petty trader…
> *Anikura*: It's a dog's life.[55]

This then dove-tails into "Who Killed Neo-Niga?", – a song which emphasizes government's uncaring attitude towards the danger which confronts the ordinary citizens on a daily basis. At the point when it attains a crescendo, "two men cross the stage", according to the stage instruction, "bearing a plain box-coffin inscribed on one side: BODY OF 1001$^{st}$ UNKNOWN VICTIM. They re-cross the stage revealing the other side of the coffin inscribed: GIFT OF TAI SOLARIN TO A CONSCIENCELESS RACE.)[56]

It seems quite necessary to pass a few comments on the technique of performance adopted by Soyinka in the play. Beside being an adaptation of one of Brecht's best known plays, there is another important sense in which Op*era Wonyosi* seems to have been influenced by Brecht. In modern dramatic practice, the avante garde German dramatist is well-accepted as the proponent of the concept of epic theatre. Brecht advertises the novel dramatic form as instructional theatre, one in which the spectator is no longer "allowed to submit to an experience

[54] ibid., 341
[55] ibid., 341 – 342
[56] ibid., 343

uncritically [. . . ] by means of simple empathy with the characters in a play."[57] One of the ways through which Brecht tried to achieve this aim was by introducing the narrator into the theatre. The narrator in this unique form of theatre introduces the play, and provides background information. He also comes in intermittently in the course of the performance to break down the play into constituent parts, to comment on the incidents just enacted, and to give a short insight into the scenes about to come. Brecht's aim in introducing this technique is so as to achieve a distancing between the spectators and the actions on stage, to prevent indeed the communicants in the theatre from losing grip of their senses, and consequently getting lost emotionally in the course of the performance. Brecht's theatre is indeed a moral theatre, and for the audience to get the message of the play, there is a need, as the dramatist insists, "to put them through a process of alienation: the alienation that is necessary to all understanding".[58]

Soyinka's narrator in *Opera Wonyosi* is the Dee-Jay and I have earlier pointed out how he comes in at the opening of the performance to introduce the play. Beside this initial appearance, Dee-Jay also appears at key moments in the course of the drama to review what has just taken place with the audience and/or give an insight into what is to come next. To cite just one more example, here is Dee-Jay at the opening of the third scene of the play:

> But you must be dying to know what's going on in the imperial crannies of Emperor Boky, otherwise known as Folksy Boksy. What preparation is he making towards his coronation? What is it that the Nigerian population in Central Afrique have not been booted out as undesirable aliens? Well, we can't answer that latter question all at once, but we can provide a link in the geographic situations. Hi Boksy, come on out, man. Stepping high if you dig the beat. Yeah – a – one, a-two, a-three, a-four; a. . .[59]

Having so generated suspense in the audience, the Dee-Jay withdraws into the wings, waiting for the next appropriate moment. Towards the end of the play, he is to step right into the middle of the action to read out Boky's special message setting Macheath free.

It seems to be the same technique of epic theatre[60] that guides Soyinka's use

[57] Bertolt Brecht, "The Modern Theatre is the Epic Theatre," in *Dramatic Theory and Criticism: Greeks to Grotowski* ed. Bernard Dukore. New York: Holt, Rinehart & Winston, 1974. p. 850

[58] Ibid. 850.

[59] *Opera Wonyosi* in *Wole Soyinka: Six Plays*, 330

[60] It is important to, at this point, qualify some of my statements on epic theatre and its influence on Soyinka. This is because most of the characteristics which Brecht articulated for the theatrical form are also found in Soyinka's Yoruba ethnic story – telling performance tradition, as they are also in several other African indigenous forms. It may therefore be a bit difficult to state with certainty whether the influence on Soyinka here derives from Brecht's epic form or from the Nigerian playwright's indigenous heritage, or both.

of songs and music in the play. Against the practice in traditional theatre where, as Brecht says, music simply "heightens the text" or, on the other hand, simply "paints the psychological situation" of the drama, in epic theatre, songs and music are meant to "communicate," move the action of the play forward and, also, "take a position." [61] In *Opera Wonyosi*, precisely in the manner stipulated by this theatre of alienation, music is an intricate part of the narration, setting forth the plot. [62] I have earlier cited the example of "Who Killed neo-Niga," a song whose lyrics puts forward government's attitude of indifference toward the plight of the ordinary citizens. Another example that I may just cite here is the very song performed at the opening of the play. Immediately after Dee Jay's introductory speech, the company comes on stage to perform the first theme, used to introduce Macheath, thus giving the spectators a picture of his character. The song paints him as a murderer, an armed robber and a professional assassin. "Where the night flows dark and silent," so goes the song in part, "There you'll find men lying dead/Was it plague that really killed them/Or a fee to Mackie paid?" [63]

A word or two, finally, on the deliberate pun in the title of the play. Written as two words, and properly accented *òpé ra*, in Yoruba means "the fool buys". Wonyosi, on the other hand, is a special brand of lace that was in vogue at the time the play was first produced in 1977. This brand of lace material was very expensive and a metre was said to go for at least five – hundred dollars. Polly procures this material for Macheath in the play as part of her attempt to make him appear decent and respectable. Macheath was in fact trying on the clothe at the time he was arrested for the first time.

At a second level, and as is well known, opera in English represents that brand of theatre in which every word is sung; and written as three words, *wón yò si* again in Yoruba literally means "to add salt to", a figurative expression for exaggeration. *Opera Wonyosi* exposes the social decadence of Nigerian society exaggerating, in the process, to a ludicrous degree.

## VIII. CRITICAL RESPONSES TO *Opera Wonyosi*

Beside the subtle sanction that the play *Opera Wonyosi* received from the state following its command performance in Ife, there were, for totally different reasons, other people who expressed critical disagreements with the play. A notable

[61] Bertolt Brecht, "The Modern Theatre is the Epic Theatre," (848)

[62] Well, Bernth Lindfors has pointed it out in "Begging Questions in Wole Soyinka's *Opera Wonyosi*" that hardly was any of the songs used in the play original, that most of the time, Soyinka simply "grafted new words onto well-known Euro-American tunes, much as Gay had done with old English airs in *The Beggar's Opera*. See Bernth Lindfors, "Begging Questions in Wole Soyinka's *Opera Wonyosi*," 151 – 152

[63] *Opera Wonyosi* in *Wole Soyinka: Six Plays*, 304

example in this regard is Biodun Jeyifo, a Marxist critic and, at the time, Senior Lecturer in literature at the University. Writing in *Positive Review*, also a journal based in the University, Jeyifo accuses Soyinka of a lack of class perspective in his approach to literature and society; and, secondly, of totally ignoring in the play, those "vital, positive points which even in the darkest times are never totally absent" in any society. [64]

To be sure, Jeyifo was, at the time, a leading member of a school of writers, critics and other intellectuals based at, or at least loosely affiliated to, Ibadan and Ife Universities and who insisted on a radical, Marxist approach to art, literature and society. To the last person, all of the members of this school were – in the main, still are – admirers of Soyinka. Most of them had close personal relationship with him, and some had actually been trained directly by the man. In his preface to *Wole Soyinka: Politics, Poetics and Postcolonialism*, his definitive study of Soyinka's works, Jeyifo had written of the role played by this group in getting Soyinka to end his four year exile in 1975 and return to Nigeria to take up an appointment as a Professor of Comparative Literature at the University of Ife. The group had actually sent Jeyifo himself and Kole Omotoso on a special mission to Ghana, where Soyinka then worked as a full-time editor of a new journal, *Transition*, and the purpose of the mission, simply, was to persuade their mentor to take a positive view of the realities at home, especially following the overthrow of the military regime of Yakubu Gowon which had, in the first place sent the man to jail. Soyinka agreed with the perspectives of his visitors. "Like us," says Jeyifo, "[Soyinka] also felt that things were looking as auspicious for 'new beginnings' as they had ever been at any other time in the fifteen years of Nigeria's post-independence history". [65] Shortly after the visit, Soyinka put an end to his multi-dimensional activities in Ghana, heading straight for Ife.

As Jeyifo confesses, nobody anticipated the direction events took soon after Soyinka's arrival in Nigeria. For, within a period of one year, and according to Jeyifo, Soyinka was said to have totally fallen out with "most leftist writers, critics and academics in the country." As the eminent leftist scholar further states, this "falling apart [...] was particularly acute between Soyinka and us, members of the Ibadan-Ife Group who had been so eager for his return from exile". [66]

In "Soyinka and His Radical Critics," Brian Crow presents an informed summary of the major points of disagreement between Soyinka and his junior friends. Crow starts by stating cogently the context of the quarrel. First, by the late 1970s, and as Crow rightly points out, Soyinka had established a reputation as the most exciting dramatist to come out of postcolonial Africa. Also, due to the position

64 Biodun Jeyifo, "Drama and the Social Order: Two Reviews". *Positive Review*, No. 1 1977, 24.

65 Biodun Jeyifo, *Wole Soyinka: Politics, Poetics and Postcolonialism*, xiii.

66 Ibid., xiii.

he took during the Nigerian civil war, and his consistently trenchant views on successive regimes in the country, the man had also become quite well – known in Nigeria, even among people who know nothing about his writings. Principally because of this factor, and also because of the fact that, and according to Crow, Soyinka also presents himself as a "revolutionary humanist socialist," the radical critics had been somewhat disappointed about the way Soyinka often presents the common run of humanity in his works. Responding to him in works after works, the critics projected Soyinka, and to use Crow's exact words "as a brilliant but ultimately reactionary romantic", [67] comparing his works unfavourably with those of other left-leaning writers from other parts of the continent. [68]

Exemplifying his position, Crow uses two critical pieces, again written by Jeyifo and published in the same *Positive Review*. The first one is a reaction to *Myth, Literature and the African World*, Soyinka's book of essays first published in 1976. Crow points out Jeyifo's positive observation regarding Soyinka's gift for in-depth analysis, the man's penetrating insight, and his supreme confidence; but how ultimately he, Jeyifo, takes issues with what he sees as Soyinka's indifference to the historical basis of his materials. In an attempt to make his readers obtain a true feel of the leftist critic's arguments, Crow quotes at length from Jeyifo's review:

> Here the explosive contradictions of the continent vanish and writers slough off their objective and subjective class sympathies and attitudes. Class perspectives are in fact completely absent in this book: ideology is seen as ... religious – secular or racial – civilisational... The matter is obvious and inescapable: in class – divided societies such as contemporary African nation – states are, as the ideological and political struggles intensify, it is one of the ruses of the dominant ideology for the ruling classes to proffer a mystificatory consensual, all-in-the-family, business as usual, harmonious 'world – view' which employs everybody. Cultural validation, 'self apprehension', undeniably an important agenda of African liberation, must free itself of this massive ideological complicity in the domination of the ruling classes of Africa. [69]

The second piece by Jeyifo which Crow uses to exemplify the radical critics' response to Soyinka is the one in which he – again Jeyifo – compares *Death and*

---

[67] Brian Crow, "Soyinka and his Radical Critics," in *Perspectives on Wole Soyinka: Freedom and Complexity* ed. Biodun Jeyifo. Jackson: University Press of Mississippi, 2001, p. 95

[68] Actually, there is another school of Nigerian critics which takes an even more uncompromising position on Soyinka's works. Led by Chinweizu, this school insists that for any works to qualify for inclusion in the corpus of African literature, it must project a separate, authentic, African aesthetics. It is based on this premise that these critics found Soyinka guilty of pandering to the dictates of Western, euro-modernist literary aesthetics. For details, see Chinweizu, et al. *Towards the Decolonization of African Literature*. Washington DC: Howard University Press, 1983.

[69] Ibid., 96

*the King's Horseman*, discussed above, with Ebrahim Hussein's *Kinjeketile*, an historical tragedy which dramatizes the history of a revolt against German colonialism in the then Southern Tanganyika (present day Tanzania). [70] Jeyifo presents Soyinka's work as a representative of the African tradition of historical tragedy, which tradition often divests tragic conflicts of their social and material contexts, reflecting them instead at the level of "categorical superstructures." Speaking specifically of *Death and the King's Horseman*, Jeyifo argues, and Crow quotes him, that in the play, Soyinka "polarizes the conflict between a traditional African, organic vision of life and an alien system of discrete laws and social polity, with tragic results for the indigenous system". By so doing, and as Jeyifo writes further, the respected playwright has suppressed "the real, objective differences between conflicting groups and classes within the indigenous system." [71]

Crow takes Jeyifo's critical position as representative of other members of his generation, including Femi Osofisan, [72] arguably postcolonial Africa's next most important playwright after Soyinka and Athol Fugard, and who often accuses Soyinka of projecting ambiguous positions in most of his plays; and Yemi Ogunbiyi who once wrote that "a committed work of art [...] must lay bare unambiguously the causal historical and socio-economic network of society". [73] Whatever the case, Soyinka replied his critics, point for point, and in the same vitriolic language. "Who is Afraid of Elesin Oba" and "The Critic and Society: Barthes, Leftocracy and other Mythologies", two of the Nobel laureate's major critical essays were devoted to this project. [74] Crow exemplifies Soyinka's position with the latter, which, actually, was the inaugural lecture he delivered at the University of Ife in 1982. The term "leftocracy" in the title of the lecture was what he used to describe the critics whom he sees as lacking a proper understanding of the ideology they seek to propagate. To the playwright, and as Crow presents his argument, for an artist to transform society, what he/she needs to do is to set free the spectators' minds "from the superstition of Power which cripples the will, obscures self-apprehension and facilitates surrender to the alienating processes ranged against every form of human productivity". [75] At the end of his essay on *Death and the*

---

70 Biodun Jeyifo, "Ideology and Tragic Epistemology: The Emergent Paradigms in Contemporary African Drama", in his *The Truthful Lie: Essays in a Sociology of African Drama*. London: New Beacon, 1985. pp. 28 – 42

71 Ibid. 34

72 See Femi Osofisan. "Wole Soyinka and a Living Dramatist," in *Wole Soyinka: An Appraisal*. Ed. Adewale Maja – Pearce. London: Heinemann, 1994.43 – 60

73 Yemi Ogunbiyi, "*Opera Wonyosi*: A Study of Soyinka's *Opera Wonyosi*", *Nigeria Magazine*, Nos 128 – 129, 1979, 3 – 14.

74 Wole Soyinka, *The Critic and Society: Barthes, Leftocracy and other Mythologies*, Inaugural Lecture Series 49 Ile – Ife, 1982

75 Brian Crow, "Soyinka and his Radical Critics," 99

*King's Horseman*, Jeyifo poses what he describes as the "lasting ideological query to art and drama: about whom; for whom?" Responding, Soyinka throws the question back at the critic, asking him to also name the targeted audience he has in mind anytime he picks up his pen to write an essay. "For, unquestionably", and as Crow quotes Soyinka:

There is an intellectual cop – out in the career of any critic who covers reams of paper with unceasing lament on the failure of this or that writer to write for the masses of the people, when he himself assiduously engages – with a remorseless exclusivity – only the incestuous productivity of his own academic – that is – bourgeois situated literature.[76]

What the foregoing demonstrates in short is that Jeyifo's review of *Opera Wonyosi* is a continuation of an on-going debate. It is in the same sense that it becomes understandable that Soyinka had to respond with the kind of serious umbrage as evidenced in the foreword he wrote to the published version of the work. While, as he says in the said forward, he is in agreement with the view that art needs to reflect the positive points of a particular historical period, the playwright contends that, equally, "it is necessary that art (also) should expose, reflect, indeed magnify the decadent, rotted underbelly of a society that has lost its direction, jettisoned all sense of values and is careering down a precipice ... "[77]. As regards the issue of class analysis, Soyinka is unequivocal in his rejection of, in his own words, the "irrational claim that a work of social criticism must submerge its expression of moral disgust for the anodyne of correct class analysis":

At the very least, the former takes the subject away from the escapist rhetoric, from conveniently remote and 'scientific' causes and rubs the faces of the collaborators – the audience – in social shame, in the sewer of their material existence. We do not intend to give any 'intellectual' audience the comfort of seeing their material situation as the *inevitable* consequence of their socio-historical condition. We pronounce: 'Guilty' on all counts, then we leave the rest to the potential re-shaping force of society – among which we, the writers, consider ourselves – to work upon.[78]

Since the early eighties, Soyinka has continued to re-explore the different dimensions of the complex themes of *Opera Wonyosi* in one satiric work after the other. With a grimly ironic title, *A Play of Giants*[79] parades the four African despots that have earlier been named as they carry their buffoonery to the United Nations headquarters in New York. *A Scourge of Hyacinth* and *From Zia with Love*[80] represent more or less one and the same play, with one being a radio version of the

76 Ibid., 98–99
77 *Opera Wonyosi* in *Wole Soyinka: Six Plays*, 298
78 Ibid., 299
79 Wole Soyinka. *A Play of Giants*. London: Methuen, 1981.
80 Wole Soyinka. *From Zia with Love and a Scourge of Hyacinths*. London: Methuen, 1992.

other. The story here enacted is based on a real life incident which took place in Nigeria in 1985. This was the time when General Muhammadu Buhari was the Head of State and the incident had to do with three people who were executed for drug trafficking offenses based on a retroactively promulgated decree. In *The Beatification of Area Boys,* [81] a wedding ceremony leads to an open confrontation between the elite and a section of the neglected citizenry. And recently premiered at the National Theatre is *King Baabu,* [82] a play which savagely attacks the recent Abacha despotism in Nigeria. Obviously to Soyinka, and as he points out in the same foreword to *Opera Wonyosi*, such exposition of the rotten underside of the society represents "a prerequisite of the land's transformation." [83]

---

[81] Wole Soyinka. *The Beatification of Area Boys*. London: Methuen, 1995

[82] Wole Soyinka. *King Baabu*. London: Methuen, 2002

[83] *Opera Wonyosi* in *Wole Soyinka: Six Plays*, 300

## WORKS CITED

Armstrong, Robert Plant. "Tragedy – Greek and Yoruba: A Cross – Cultural Perspective," *Research in African Literature*, 7 (1976), pp. 23 – 43

Beier, Ulli. *Orisa Liberates the Mind: Wole Soyinka in Conversation with Ulli Beier on Yoruba Religions*. Bayreuth: Iwalewa, 1992

Brecht Bertolt. "The Modern Theatre is the Epic Theatre," in *Dramatic Theory and Criticism: Greeks to Grotowski* ed. Bernard Dukore. New York: Holt, Rinehart & Winston, 1974 pp. 847 – 854

Brecht, Bertolt. *The Threepenny Opera*. London: Eyre Methuen. 1979

Chinweizu, et al *Towards the Decolonization of African Literature*. Washington DC: Howard University, Press, 1993

Crow, Brian. "Soyinka and his Radical Critics," in *Perspectives on Wole Soyinka: Freedom and Complexity* ed. Biodun Jeyifo. Jackson: University Press of Mississippi, 2001

Etherton, Michael. *The Development of African Drama*. London: Hutchinson University Library of Africa. 1982

Fugard, Athol. *Statements: Three Plays*. London: Oxford University Press, 1974

Gay, John.*The Beggars' Opera*. New York: Dover Publications. 1973

Gibbs, James & Bernth Lindfors (eds.) *Research on Wole Soyinka*. Trenton, NJ: Africa World Press, 1993

Gibbs, James. *Wole Soyinka*. London: Macmillans. 1986

Hinton, Stephen (Ed.). *Kurt Weill: The Threepenny Opera*. Cambridge: Cambridge University Press.

Irele, Abiola. "Tradition and the Yoruba Writer: D.O. Fagunwa, Amos Tutuola & Wole Soyinka," in *The African Experience in Literature and Ideology*. Bloomington IN: Indiana, University Press, 1990. pp. 174 – 197

Jeyifo Biodun ed. *Perspectives on Wole Soyinka: Freedom and Complexity*. Jackson: University Press of Mississippi, 2001

Jeyifo, Biodun. "Drama and the Social Order: Two Reviews", in *Positive Review*, No. 1 1977.

Jeyifo, Biodun. *The Truthful Lie: Essays in a Sociology of African Drama*. London: New Beacon, 1985

Jeyifo, Biodun. *Wole Soyinka: a Voice from Africa*. New York. IMG Educators. 1990

Jeyifo, Biodun. *Wole Soyinka: Politics, Poetics and Postcolonialism*. Cambridge: Cambridge University, Press, 2004

Jones, Eldred Durosimi. *The Writing of Wole Soyinka*. London: James Currey. 1988

Larsen Stephan. *A Writer and his Gods: A Study of the Importance of Myths and*

*Religious Ideas to the Writings of Wole Soyinka*. Stockholm: University of Stockholm Department of the History of Literature, 1993

Lindfors Bernth. "Begging Questions in Wole Soyinka's *Opera Wonyosi*" in *Research on Wole Soyinka* ed. James Gibbs & Bernth Lindfors. Trenton, NJ: Africa World Press, 1993. pp. 149 – 159

Maja – Pearce, Adewale (ed.). *Wole Soyinka: An Appraisal*. London: Heinemann, 1994

Nasiru, Akanji. "Ola Rotimi's Search for Technique," in *Introduction to West African Literature* ed. Kolawole Ogungbesan. Ibadan: Ibadan University Press, 1979. pp. 62 73

Ogunba, Oyin. "Traditional African Festival Drama," in Oyin Ogunba & Abiola Irele (Eds.) *Theatre in Africa*. Ibadan: Ibadan University Press, 1978 pp. 3 – 26

Ogunbiyi, Yemi. "Opera Wonyosi: a Study of Soyinka's *Opera Wonyosi*.", in *Nigeria Magazine*, Nos 128 – 129, 1979, pp. 3 – 14.

Olaniyan, Tejumola. *Scars of Conquest/Masks of Resistance: the Invention of Cultural Identity in African, African American & Caribbean Drama*. New York: Oxford University Press, 1995

Osofisan, Femi. "Wole Soyinka and a Living Dramatist: A Playwright's Encounter with Soyinka's Drama," in *Wole Soyinka: An Appraisal* ed. Adewale Maja – Pearce. London: Heinemann, 1994 pp. 43 – 60

Rotimi, Ola. *The Gods are not to Blame*. London: Oxford University Press. 1971

Sophocles. *The Theban Plays*. Harmondsworth: Penguin 1981

Soyinka, Wole *King Baabu*. London:Methuen, 2002

Soyinka, Wole. "The Lysistrata of Aristophanes", in *Art, Dialogue and Outrage: Essays on African Literature and Culture*. Ibadan: New Horn. 1988 pp. 35 – 41.

Soyinka, Wole. *A Play of Giants*. London: Methuen. 1984

Soyinka, Wole. *From Zia with Love and A Scourge of Hyacinths*. London: Methuen. 1992

Soyinka, Wole. *Myth, Literature and the African World*. Cambridge: Cambridge University Press, 1976

Soyinka, Wole.*Opera Wonyosi*. London: Rex Collins. 1981

Soyinka, Wole. *Requiem for a Futurologist*. London: Rex Collins. 1985

Soyinka, Wole. *Soyinka: Collected Plays I*. Oxford: Oxford University Press, 1973

Soyinka, Wole. *Soyinka: Six Plays*. London: Methuen, 1992

Soyinka, Wole. *The Beatification of Area Boys*. London: Methuen. 1995.

Soyinka, Wole. *The Critic and Society: Barthes, Leftocracy and Other Mythologies*. Inaugural Lecture Series 49 Ile Ife, 1982

Willet, John (ed.). *Brecht on Theatre. The Development of an Aesthetic*. London: Eyre Methuen. 1964.

Winton, Calhoun. *John Gay and the London Theatre*. Kentucky: The University Press of Kentucky. 1993.

# CHAPTER 2

# DREAM SEEKER AND THE DIVINIG CHAIN: PRELIMINARY REMARKS ON AN AFRICAN DRAMATIST OF THE SECOND GENERATION[1]

## I: SETTING OUT

Femi Osofisan has now been writing for over thirty years. *The Chattering and the Song*, his first important play, was first published in 1976, initiating with it a new direction in African dramatic tradition. Arguably. As suggested by its title, this chapter represents a tentative exploration of the oeuvre of this particular dramatist. It assesses his development as a dramatist, the assumptions that power his works as well as the salient issues in his thematic and stylistic articulations. In short, the chapter examines Osofisan's achievements in the past three decades or so and locates a place for him in African theatre history.

## II: TAKING OFF

Few theatre historians seem to have acknowledged it but 1976 and 1977 stand as landmark years in the development of African drama. 1976 it was when Ngugi wa Thiong'o, collaborating with Micere Mugo, undertook a reconstruction of the history of Dedan Kimathi, the man who led the Mau Mau struggle for independence in the fifties through the sixties in Kenya in a dramatic work titled *The Trial of Dedan Kimathi*[2]. The play was eventually accepted as Kenya's entry for drama in the World Black Festival of Arts and Culture (FESTAC) held in Lagos in 1977, along with Francis Imbuga's *Betrayal in the City.* But perhaps more important were the controversial pre-festival productions[3] which took place in the

---

1 An earlier version of this chapter was published with a slightly different title in *Ilorin Journal of Language and Literature* (IJLL):Vol. 4: 17 – 28

2 See Ngugi wa Thiong'o & Micere Mugo, *The Trial of Dedan Kimathi*. (London: Heinemann, 1976)

3 The controversy was between Ngugi and the FESTAC '77 Drama Group on the one hand, and the management of Kenyan National Theatre who were mainly expatriates, on the other. The point of contention had been on what plays to put up at the Kenya Cultural Centre during the "Kenyatta Day" week of 1976. While the authorities had preferred two foreign entries – *James*

Kenyan National Theatre between October 20 and 30, 1976. So successful were the performances that the audiences spilled into the streets each night chanting the politically explosive songs in the play. Ngugi was however to leave the play behind soon after its production in Lagos in 1977 as the activist writer found himself as a participant in the community development efforts of the people of Kamirithu, then a village of about 11,000 inhabitants located in the Limuru district of Kenya. *Ngaahika Ndeenda* (translated as *I will Marry When I Want)* [4] represents an even greater achievement being, as it were, a veritable example of theatre as a reflection of, and guide for, national life and national culture. [5]

But while all this was going on in Kenya, a more or less parallel development was taking place in Nigeria. At the centre of this group which was proposing a radical perspective of art and society was, among others, Femi Osofisan, then a young man of thirty and a lecturer in the Department of Modern European Languages, University of Ibadan.

Osofisan had actually started off as a disciple of Wole Soyinka. In tracing the origins of Modern West African drama in the doctoral dissertation he submitted to the University of Ibadan two years earlier, the young man had, indeed, followed the thesis proposed by Soyinka in his seminal essay "The Fourth Stage". And in *A Restless Run of Locusts,* [6] a play first crafted in the sixties, Osofisan's preoccupation is that of individual heroism. Precisely, as Olu Obafemi has noted in *Cultural Heritage and Social Vision in Contemporary Nigerian Theatre* [7], a doctoral dissertation submitted to the University of Leeds in 1981, the play ends on a note of fatalism, again much like Soyinka. Sanda Adeniyi, the hero of the play, having betrayed an oath, willingly surrenders himself for punishment, contending

---

*Ballet de France* and *A Funny Thing Happened on the Way to the Forum* – their argument being that the organizers had booked the Centre several months in advance and that African plays did not often appeal to regular patrons of the theatre, Ngugi and his colleagues had insisted, on the other hand, on the country's two entries for the festival to be held in Nigeria. As the argument heated up and spilled into the newspapers, the Ministry of Social services which set up the FESTAC Drama Group came out to intervene and the two entries eventually won four nights each between October 20 and 30 crammed, as it were, between two foreign shows. For further details, see Ngugi wa Thiong'o, *Writers in Politics.* (London: Heinemann, 1981).

4 Ngugi wa Thiong'o & Ngugi wa Mirii, *I will Marry when I Want.* (London: Heinemann, 1982)

5 For further discussion of this play, see Wumi Raji, "Transformed Identities: Cultural Transgression and Postcolonial Transformation in Ngugi wa Thiong'o and Ngugi wa Mirii's *I Will Marry when I Want.*" *Journal of Contemporary Drama in English,* 11: 25 – 39, Ngugi wa Thiong'o, *Detained: A Writer's Prison Diary.* (London: Heinemann, 1981), Ngugi wa Thiong'o, *Writers in Politics.* (London: Heinemann, 1981), and Ingrid Bjorkman, *Mother Sing for Me: People's Theatre in Kenya.* (London: Zed Books, 1989)

6 Femi Osofisan, *A Restless Run of Locusts.* (Ibadan: New Horn, 1975)

7 Olu Obafemi, "Cultural Heritage and Social Vision in Contemporary Nigerian Theatre." (Unpublished Doctoral Thesis, University of Leeds, 1981)

that "the only real way we can be true to ourselves is by keeping our date with destiny"[8] (52).

## III: THE PARTING OF WAYS

1976 was the year when Osofisan announced his departure from Soyinka, linking up now with Biodun Jeyifo, Kole Omotoso, Niyi Osundare, Ropo Sekoni, Bode Sowande and others to propose a radical alternative of literature and society. In "Ritual and Revolutionary Ethos," the paper he presented that year at the First Ibadan Annual African Literature Conference, Osofisan launches an attack on the dramatic perspective of his predecessor and mentor. Taking apart *The Strong Breed*[9] and *Death and the King's Horseman,*[10] the two plays of Soyinka that he uses to illustrate his argument, the young playwright declares as anachronistic, an unmediated and untreated mythical perspective of art and society suggesting that "in order to adequately come to terms with the rapacious dehumanized white men of Europe and America, the ancient modes of life must... yield place to an empiric mastery of life"[11]. Even as he presented his paper at the conference, Osofisan had already completed work on *The Chattering and the Song*, arguably the first important radical play in Nigeria.

The activities of 1976 were intensified in 1977. Earlier in May of the latter year, Biodun Jeyifo, Femi Osofisan's close friend and ideological ally had presented a polemic criticism of Soyinka's *Death and the King's Horseman* comparing it with Ebrahim Hussein's *Kinjeketile* in "Ideology and Tragic Epistemology: the Emergent Paradigms in Contemporary African Drama"[12] at the University of Ife Modern European Languages Departmental seminars. And as a follow up to *The Chattering and the Song*, Osofisan made sure he completed work on *Who Is Afraid of Solarin*, a satirical comedy adapted from Nikolai Gogol's *The Government Inspector*, on time for the first and only workshop so far on "Radical Perspective in African Literature and Society" which was held in December of that year. Soyinka himself had, at that conference, come face to face with the

---

8 *A Restless Run of Locusts*, 52

9 Wole Soyinka, *The Strong Breed*, in Wole Soyinka: *Collected Plays I*. (Oxford: oxford University Press, 1973): 113–146

10 Wole Soyinka, *Death and the King's Horseman* in *Soyinka: Six Plays*, (London: Methuen, 1984): 165–252

11 Femi Osofisan, *The Nostalgic Drum: Essays on Literature, Drama and Culture*. (Trenton, NJ: Africa World Press, 2001): 97

12 See Biodun Jeyifo, "Ideology and Tragic Epistemiology: The Emergent Paradigms in Comtemporary Nigerian Theatre," in Biodun Jeyifo, *The Truthful Lie: Essays in a Sociology of African Drama*. (London: New Beacon, 1985)

young writers and critics to declare the end of his patience "with (the) would be demagogues of chic radicalism". [13]

## IV: DISCURSIVE PARADIGM

"Drama and the New Exotic: The Paradox of Form in Modern African Theatre" [14], represents one of the most intellectually rigorous background discourse to radical theatre in Nigeria. The paper, written, again, by Femi Osofisan, was first presented in 1978 at the Literature Seminar of the Department of Modern European Languages, University of Ife. The essay commences by admitting that Soyinka, Rotimi, Sutherland and Oyono Mbia stand as masters of the modern stage in Africa. The works of the four playwrights, according to Osofisan, share two qualities in common: "immense popularity with differing audiences, and secondly, a questionable recidivist celebration of culture, the glamour of the New Exotic." [15] From this we begin to glean the meaning of the central term in the discourse: the New Exotic.

As Osofisan admits, the greatest struggle a dramatist experiences in the creative process is the one undertaken to control the tension between content and form. From the point of view of the modern progressive, however, it would seem that the dramatist now concentrates more attention on form to the detriment of content. The result of this, says Osofisan, is a socially reactionary theatre opposed paradoxically to a highly infectious form:

> The theatre of the New Exotic would be an immensely seductive theatre, effortlessly drawing a large clientele which cut across socio-economic classes. But that success would lead to no illumination or epiphany, to no spiritual fulfillment [16]

Osofisan locates the roots of the new exotic in Negritude, a philosophy of authentication of an indigenous African worldview, which developed in the fifties in the French speaking colonies as a reaction against the racist assumptions of the colonial masters. The aim of Negritude, the articulation of an original African civilization, soon found an articulate platform in the theatre. Thus it happens that, in the Francophone African world, the theatre projected only the ancient African order, the great courts of Sudan, Congo and Guinea. The emperors, long dead, and as Osofisan contends in the essay, were exhumed and restored to their thrones, together with their slaves and serfs, their harems and drummers and praise singers.

---

13 Wole Soyinka, "Who is Afraid of Elesin Oba." In *Wole Soyinka: Art, Dialogue and Outrage* (Ibadan: New Horn, 1986): 23

14 Femi Osofisan, "Drama and the New Exotic: The Paradox of Form in Modern African Theatre." In *African Theatre Review* Vol 1, No 1: 72 – 84

15 *African Theatre Review*, 76

16 *African Theatre Review*, 79

This continued for a very long time, according to Osofisan, the theme of the Old Exotic, where the dramatist focused his gaze permanently on the day before, just to show that his people used to possess a great civilization. It continued until *Une Saison au Congo and Chant hater la Mort du temps Orphee* when dramatists like Cesaire, Boukman and Nokan rejected Senghor for Frantz Fanon, Amilcar Cabral and Ahmed Sekou Toure, among others.

As Osofisan insists, the Anglophone African World initially rejected Negritude in all its ramifications, maintaining, as Soyinka does, that "a tiger does not shout its tigritude, it acts". Of course, the master himself, Soyinka that is, had already written *A Dance of the Forests* to demonstrate that the African past was not without its own ambiguities and contradictions. He had followed this up with other plays that focus sharply on the present like the *The Road*, *Before the Blackout* and others. Ola Rotimi had his satirical comedy *Our Husband Has Gone Mad Again* and Efua Sutherland *Anowa.* Soon after this, however, the Anglophone playwrights themselves began to experience a slide. They began to move away from their critical realist position towards the New Exotic. The tendency, according to Osofisan, is demonstrated in Soyinka's *Death and the King's Horseman,* Ola Rotimi's *The Gods are not to Blame* and Efua Sutherland's *The Marriage of Anansewa.* In all of these plays, and as Osofisan contends, we find writers moving back to their original culture and exploiting their resources of dance, drama and poetry to produce works of great vitality. As he further maintains, "the pervasive elements of culture, as authentic and enchanting as they may be, are present (in these plays) more often as ornamentation and décor than as catalytic element of critical examination, more as data of information than of evaluation and exploited for the purposes of visceral dramatic effect than for an intellectual or even spiritual compact with history" [17]. As to how to resolve this paradox of what Osofisan describes as the New Exotic, precisely how to "create exciting theatre upon a critical relationship with indigenous culture," Osofisan suggests that the African playwrights of the generation after Soyinka "are already seeking answers." [18]

The answers which these playwrights have presumably proposed are demonstrated by a profusion of plays articulating a dialectical materialist perspective of art and society. These plays include Femi Osofisan's *The Chattering and the Song*, *Once Upon Four Robbers, Morountodun*, *Another Raft*, *Yungba Yungba and the Dance Contest*, *Eshu and the Vagabond Minstrels*, *Red Is the Freedom Road*, *No More the Wasted Breed*, among others, Kole Omotoso's *The Curse* and *Shadows in the Horizon*, Bode Sowande's *Farewell to Babylon*, *Flamingo*, *Afamako* and *Tornadoes Full of Dreams* and Olu Obafemi's *The New Dawn*, *Nights of a*

[17] *African Theatre Review*, 81
[18] *African Theatre Review*, 85

*Mystical Beast* and *Suicide Syndrome*. That the list is dominated by the works of Osofisan is clearly inevitable since, arguably, he represents the most prolific, the most sophisticated and the most engaging of all of the playwrights.

## V: ENGAGEMENT: A FORMULA

Directly, there are three broad points of departure in Osofisan's dramatic output: the demystification [19] of the theatrical idiom, the destabilization of hegemonic constructs and the empowerment of the ordinary people.

By demystification, I refer to the various methods adopted by Osofisan to dismantle the conventional notion of theatre as alternative reality. Almost right from the moment of take – off, and deriving inspiration simultaneously from his indigenous heritage as well as the theoretical writings and dramatic output of Bertolt Brecht, the German avante garde dramatist, Osofisan has made his goals that of destabilizing the received definition of theatre as a "willing suspension of disbelief". Theatre, as he often vehemently argues, is no more than "mere artifice" packaged for the audience's "entertainment" but which of course contains some measure of truth designed for the purpose of preparing the same spectators for life's actualities. Osofisan is never tired of drumming this into his audience's ears and of course through various means and methods. In *The Chattering and the Song* for example, the spectators are told, long before – hand that another play would be enacted within the one being watched. This other play which has been assembled to mark the wedding ceremony holding between two of the characters ultimately takes off with the actors and actresses assuming their new roles right in the full glare of the audience and with makeshift costumes and props arranged almost on the spur of the moment. The stage instruction reads partly:

> During this play we must feel the characters especially Sontri at first searching for words and attitudes, until they gradually, if unconsciously, merge with the figures they are trying to impersonate. One possible way of showing this would be in the change of verbal rhythms and tonation. Now, as the reading gathers momentum, Funlola begins to reposition objects in the room in more appropriate places, even changing lights, till the scene begins to approximate the actual setting of the drama: i.e a room in ancient Yoruba palace circa 1885 [20]

---

[19] Olu Obafemi first used this word to describe the works of Femi Osofisan together with those of his (Osofisan) like – minded contemporaries. Obafemi's employment of the term however is in its conventional sense: the abrogation or subversion of all forms of mysticism and/or mythology in drama and theatre. See his essay "Towards the Popularisation and Demystification of the Theatrical Medium for Revolutionary Aims in Africa." Unpublished manuscript.

[20] *The Chattering and the Song*, 34

Osofisan is to polish up this technique in subsequent plays of his. Thus it happens that *Once Upon Four Robbers* [21] opens like a traditional tale presented under the moonlight with the action of the drama itself appearing like the accompanying enactments to the storyteller's narration. *Morountodun* [22] commences with Director coming on stage to announce, not just the opening of a play, but also to provide the audience with a historical background to the story which is about to be acted out. The same character is to show up to provide intermittent commentary in the course of the performance.

Another dimension to this act of demystification, which needs to be spelt out in some details, is underscored by Osofisan himself in a 1986 interview with Muyiwa Awodiya. In the said interview which has now been included in the book of interviews with Osofisan, *Excursions in Drama and Theatre,* [23] Osofisan characterizes Soyinka as a playwright in the classical sense; by which he means that the Nobel Laureate simply crafts his plays without giving any thought to their staging viability especially in the African context. To be sure, this statement is true not only of Soyinka but also of many other dramatists of his generation including, especially, J.P. Clark. Osofisan, on the other hand, has worked away from these predecessors of his as he attempts to "pioneer new patterns of dramaturgy" that will not demand any "technical complexity" [24] In fact, quite a number of his plays, especially the ones created since *Morountodun* require only the empty space and of course the players. In *Yungba-Yungba and the Dance Contest,* [25] in *Farewell to a Cannibal Rage,* [26] in *Eshu and the Vagabond Minstrels* [27] and in *Another Raft,* [28] we see this quality demonstrated quite clearly.

The playwright is particularly blatant about it in the last example, a work that has all the potentials of being difficult since it represents an engagement of J.P. Clark's naturalistic script, *The Raft*. This latter play is set on a creek in the Niger Delta with four lumbermen sailing on a raft down the river. The stage instruction at the beginning of act one reads as follows:

Night on a creek in the Niger Delta. In the milky light, the shadow of a cabin is squatting on a raft (which may as well be the board or stage itself). Through the rear end of the cabin showing a cross section like a pyramid and a shade darker, one or two figures can

---

21 *Femi Osofisan, Once Upon Four Robbers*. (Ibadan: Heinemann Educational Books, 1991)

22 *Femi Osofisan, Morountodun and other Plays*. (Lagos: Longman, 1982)

23 Muyiwa Awodiya (ed.), *Excursions in Drama and Theatre: Interviews with Femi Osofisan*. (Lagos: Kraft Books, 1993)

24 *Excursions in Drama and Theatre*, 67

25 Femi Osofisan, *Yungba Yungba and the Dance Contest*. (Ibadan: Heinemann Educational Books, 1993)

26 Femi Osofisan,*Farewell to a Cannibal Rage* (Ibadan: Heinemann Educational Books, 1992)

27 Femi Osofisan, *Eshu and the Vagabond Minstrel*. ( Ibadan: Heineman Educational Books, 1991)

28 Femi Osofisan, *Another Raft*. (Lagos: Malthouse, 1988)

be seen lying about, half asleep and with yet an inner shade of dark to them. Above them flickers a lamp [29]

In Osofisan's re-writing of the play, the spectators are warned right from the beginning that they are in the theatre, the house of imaginative performance, and that in such a place, nothing is real, and can be real. So there will be no pretence, no attempt at approximating actuality. It is necessary to reproduce the words of Yemosa One, if only for the purpose of comparison with the stage instruction lifted from Clark's original play:

> You see, we need a raft here for our story, on which some of the characters will soon be making a journey. But who has ever heard of a real raft inside a building like this?... No, there's no need to deceive you, you're all intelligent people. These mats, that's all you'll see. Just plain make-belief: Look at them, fill the rest with your imagination, and with no difficulty at all, you'll see a raft floating on the waters! [30]

To Clark, everything must be as natural as possible. His producer must strain him/herself to achieve this, he or she will have to construct not just a cabin but one complete with a cross section resembling a pyramid. And since the action is supposed to be taking place in the night, he will also have to produce a lamp. It does not matter, of course, that the stage will be fully illuminated with the aids of modern electronic gadgets.

Osofisan raises a resounding objection against this. Theatre may be a dream but it is one with its eyes wide open. It is indeed nothing but a lie, a fairy tale. What matters, as he therefore contends, was not the technical paraphernalia but the resourcefulness and skills of the players.

Which leads us to the second point. Because Yemosa One, whose speech is quoted above is a sea goddess. And such characters as goddesses, gods, legendary personages, priests and such others represent the most prevalent metaphors of hegemony in the works of Osofisan. Again, in another interview with Awodiya, Osofisan reiterates his well-known position to the effect that one reason why these characters keep on recurring in his works is because he sees them as representing images of identity. "There are no people in this world without gods," he argues. "It's a way of explaining themselves and their relationship to the world, to the universe, to history." [31] But it is clear to the playwright that history itself is not static, that the universe is dynamic. This is why he advocates an attitude of challenge, of skepticism and of iconoclasm vis-à-vis these characters. Once more,*The Chattering and the Song,* comes in handy. I have already hinted at it that the

[29] J.P. Clark, *Three Plays.* (Ibadan: Oxford University Press, 1964): 91

[30] *Another Raft*, 3

[31] *Excursions in Drama and Literature,* 80

play-within-the play is a transformation of an aspect of the history of Oyo as it happened in 1885. Alaafin Abiodun, from the perspective of dominant tradition, stands as one of the most charismatic rulers of ancient Oyo. He, in fact, it was who enjoyed the reputation of checking the pestilence that Bashorun Gaha, the then Prime Minister of Oyo empire eventually constituted himself into. Abiodun consolidated this victory by afterwards establishing a benevolent regime in the land. The story of the confrontation between Abiodun and Gaha is the subject of a brilliant play written by Adebayo Faleti. *Bashorun Gaha,* [32] as it is appropriately titled, foregrounds a stiff contest of will and authority which inevitably leads to the defeat and destruction of Bashorun Gaha and the consequent entrenchment of Abiodun.

Osofisan is clearly dissatisfied with Faleti's transformation of this historical text, this affirmation of a dominant perspective of tradition. "Always" he says in an interview with Olu Obafemi, "we present history as it if was one monolithic thing, as if there was never any challenge to power in the past, as if the society never questioned itself" [33]. So, in his own attempt at dismantling the hegemonic assumptions of the earlier narrative, Osofisan focuses on the aspect of the opposition sponsored by Latoye, Gaha's only surviving son, against Abiodun. Historically, Latoye's dissidence was feeble and ineffective, favoured as it were neither by history nor by circumstance. But Osofisan rearranges the whole text in *The Chattering and the Song.* Alaafin Abiodun comes out as a despotic ruler and Latoye as a powerful, courageous and articulate opponent. The play brings the two together in an open confrontation and Latoye, mobilizing the palace guards against the throne undercuts Alaafin Abiodun.

Of course, Osofisan's ultimate aim in destabilizing hegemonies is to empower ordinary people. This, exactly, is how the second and the third points inter – link. The palace guards who are representative of the oppressed humanity desert Alaafin Abiodun and pitch camps with Latoye, the liberator. A similar thing happens in *Morountodun,* a play which dispels the popular perspective of the Moremi narrative. Once properly understood as a champion of the ruling class, the heroic personage has to vacate the stage for Titubi, the lady who commits class suicide to identify with farmers and peasants. The gun comes out in the play as a physical symbolization of empowerment. Titubi hands it over to Marshal, one of the leaders of the farmers' struggles, and Superintendent Salami and Alhaja Kabirat, two representatives of the bourgeois class have no choice than to surrender.

Another relevant example is *Yungba-Yungba and the Dance Contest.* Here, Iyeneri has been a priestess for a long time, so long, in fact, as for the office to

[32] Adebayo Faleti, *Basorun Gaa.* (Ibadan: Onibonoje Press, 1972)

[33] *Excursions in Drama and Literature*, 28

have been assumed as her birthright. Investigations by some of the maidens reveal, however, that Iyeneri is only a usurper. The usual attitude, of course, is to resist upon being confronted. But because the people are now mobilized, Iyeneri has no choice but to yield ground in the end. *Yungba-Yungba* clearly serves as a veritable parable on dictators and dictatorship in Africa.

In brief then, the above outlines represent Osofisan's points of departure as a dramatist. And, everything taken together, there is no doubt that Osofisan demonstrates a profound understanding of, and a complex engagement with, the plight of the different sections of the Nigerian masses, be they (dis)located in the rural areas or the urban centers. His works focus particularly on the impact on the people of an alienating social order and their simultaneous reactions and adjustments to this reality. The dramatist also engages the people's traditions and lifestyles, holding up their positive aspects as alternatives to the chaos and violence of an all consuming ideology of an emergent but totally rapacious capitalism.

## VI: WHERE IS THY BASE?

Paradoxically, the above analysis also throws up what several critics have perceived as the greatest weakness of Osofisan as a radical dramatist. Indeed, as David Cook points out by way of digression in "Soyinka: The Potentially Popular Playwright" [34] an article published in *Before Our Very Eyes,* a book of essays on Wole Soyinka which is edited by Dapo Adelugba, the general belief is that the social challenge of the body of Osofisan's plays can be fulfilled only "out there in the streets and in villages." [35] The playwright, on the other hand, has continuously insisted that his audience is university based and has consequently refused to transcend his petit-bourgeois location as an artist of the ivory tower. The inevitable result of this disjuncture between the artists and his audience is what has been perceived by a number of scholars of Osofisan as an acute feeling of alienation on the part of the playwright. To be sure, since about the middle of 1980s, the playwright has in numerous interviews talked about a "mediation" of perspective and a position that has "undergone a kind of subtle shading". Says he, in 1988, to Olu Obafemi:

> I will say that at the beginning, the anger was very much on top of my mind, anger at what was going on, and hence my writing tends to be directed at denunciation, to a literature of angry voices. But nowadays, what is paramount on my mind is not so much the anger but how to move on to something positive. To explore how we bring about that change. [36]

---

[34] David Cook, "Soyinka: The Potentially Popular Playwright." In *Before Our Very Eyes* ed. Dapo Adelugba. (Ibadan: Spectrum Books, 1987)

[35] "The Potentially Popular Playwright," 89

[36] *Excursions in Drama and Literature*, 87

It is definitely unnecessary trying to see whether such early plays as *Morountodun, The Chattering and the Song* and *Once Upon Four Robbers* can be considered as strident expressions of anger. In my own view, they are not. What I suspect though is that Osofisan has never really subscribed to the conventional perspective of a revolutionary and that the evidence presented to us by the above cited plays may only be taken as part of a process of self discovery. Indeed, what comes out from a 1986 conversation again with Muyiwa Awodiya is the picture of a playwright who has always abhorred violence in whatever form. In the said interview, Osofisan takes time to denounce Ogun, the Yoruba god of war and revolution. For too long, as he argues, our writers have focused on this god, especially his "warring leadership role". [37] For him, this is nothing but an obsession with "the myth of power", a phenomenon which in actuality represents "a major problem with our civilization". [38] People talk endlessly about the man of power, continues Osofisan, as if "there are no other people in this country" [39] who have made and are still making meaningful contribution towards growth and development. To him therefore, it is high time the Ogun image was displaced and that of Ifa held up in its place.

Osofisan dwells at length on the significance of the Yoruba divinatory system. To him, the Ifa corpus serves as the repository of knowledge; scientific, medicinal, mathematical, historical and more. What this means in essence and in Osofisan's words, is that there was a cult that interested itself in (the) gathering and storing (of) knowledge [40] and the modern philosopher and/or intellectual would do well not just to take interest in this principle but also to propagate it as a metaphor of continuous quest (and continuous hunger) for knowledge. It is time we quoted him at some length:

> I got fed up with this Ogun image which concentrates all the time on the power lust, on the adventures of warriors, how heroic it is to slaughter people but (which) teaches nothing about the exploration of knowledge. So I had to look elsewhere and I found out that all these were already in the Ifa cult. Exploration, reflection, research and philosophy are all inside it. Even statistics the primary thing-mathematics is in it. All the fundamental things about knowledge...It was like studying philosophy in the old University system, where you learnt logic, mathematics, literature, history, everything. That is what Ifa was: a comprehensive body of philosophy. So I thought then it was time to begin to emphasize this. [41]

---

[37] *Excursions in Drama and Literature*, 68

[38] *Excursions in Drama and Literature*, 68

[39] *Excursions in Drama and Literature*, 69

[40] *Excursions in Drama and Literature*, 69

[41] *Excursions in Drama and Literature*, 70

With the above, it should be getting clear why Osofisan has continued to draw back from practical political participation. Since he possesses a primarily intellectual vision, the University seems to be his appropriate location. Again, it is important that the artist's potentials even at this level is not under – rated. Because the aim, even of the most revolutionary play, can only be to arrest his audience's mind and persuade same to a particular course of action. And, available at any given University, and at most periods of time are thousands of particularly impressionable minds. Even if this is difficult to measure, it is not impossible, if it is assumed that he has been quite effective with his divining chains, [42] that Osofisan has successfully engaged many of these minds.

Be that as it may, there is no doubt that Osofisan has made very solid contributions to African theatre. He stands arguably as the most endowed, the most energetic and the most articulate of all of his contemporaries of radical orientation. Though of varying qualities, his theatrical output remains, by any standard, awesome. A consistent experimentalist, he has continued to push further the limits of his own point of departure in scripts after scripts. Niyi Osundare, poet, scholar and Osofisan's friend of many years, in a 1980 review in *West Africa* of *Once Upon Four Robbers* enthusiastically declares that "Osofisan is already on the way to doing for us (Africans) what Bertolt Brecht did for Europe." [43] This statement remains perhaps the boldest of all attempts at locating Osofisan's place in theatre history.

[42] The divining chain, described by Osofisan as "a metal or string at the tail end of which eight halves of the nuts of Opele palm tree have been sown, four at each end," is the instrument with which the Ifa priest among the Yorubas divines the problem of his client. In his second book of poems, *Dream – Seeker on Divining Chain*, a para – phrase of which has been adopted in the first half of the title of this essay, Osofisan admits that "the journey of these poems is facilitated by Ifa, but certainly not restricted to, or governed by, it. See "A Brief Notice." In *Dream – Seeker on Divining Chain*. (Lagos: Kraft Books Limited, 1993): 7 – 8

[43] Niyi Osundare, "Social Message of a Nigerian Playwright." *West Africa*, (January 28, 1980): 150

## WORKS CITED

Awodiya, Muyiwa, *Excursions in Drama and Literature: Interviews with Femi Osofisan.* (Lagos: Kraft Books, 1993).

Bjorkman, Ingrid. *Mother Sing for Me: People's Theatre in Kenya.* (London: Zed Books, 1989).

Clark. J.P., *Three Plays.* (Ibadan: Oxford University Press, 1964).

Cook, David "Soyinka: The Potentially Popular Playwright", in *Before Our Very Eyes: Tribute to Wole Soyinka* ed. Dapo Adelugba. (Ibadan: Spectrum Books, 1987).

Faleti, Adebayo, *Basorun Gaa.* (Ibadan: Onibonoje Press, 1972).

Obafemi, Olu, "Cultural Heritage and Social Vision in Contemporary Nigerian Theatre". (Unpublished Doctoral Thesis, University of Leeds, 1981).

– "Towards the Popularization of the Theatrical Medium Revolutionary Aims in Africa." (Unpublished Manuscript)

Osofisan, Femi, *Another Raft.* (Lagos: Malthouse, 1988).

– *The Chattering and the Song* Ibadan: Ibadan University Press, 1977.

– "Drama and the New Exotic: The Paradox of Form in Modern African Theatre" *African Theatre Review* Vol. 1, No. 1: 72 – 84

– *Dream – Seeker on Divining Chain.* (Lagos: Kraft Books, 1993)

– *Eshu and the Vagabond Minstrels* (Ibadan: New Horn, 1991).

– *Morountodun and Other Plays.* (Lagos: Longman, 1982).

– *Once Upon Four Robbers.* (Ibadan: Heinemann Educational Books, 1991)

– *A Restless Run of Locusts* (Ibadan: New Horn, 1975)

– "Ritual and Revolutionary Ethos" in *The Nostalgic Drum: Essays on African Literature, Drama and Culture.* Femi Osofisan. (Trenton, NJ: Africa World Press, 2001)

– *Yungba-Yungba and the Dance Contest* (Ibadan: Heinemann Educational Books, 1993).

Osundare, Niyi. "Social Message of a Nigerian Playwright" *West Africa.* (Jan. 28, 1980):. 147 – 150.

Raji, Wumi "Transformed Identities: Cultural Transgression and Postcolonial Transformation in Ngugi wa Thiong'o & Ngugi wa Mirii's I will Marry when I Want." In *Journal of Contemporary Drama in English,* 11: 25 – 39

Soyinka, Wole. "Who is Afraid of Elesin Oba" in *Art, Dialogue and Outrage* (Ibadan: New Horn, 1986).

Wa Thiong'o, Ngugi. *Detained: A Writer's Prison Diary.* (London: Heinemann, 1981)

– *Writers in Politics.* (London: Heinemann, 1981)

Wa Thiongo, Ngugi and Mugo, Micere. *The Trial of Dedan Kimathi* (London: Heinemann, 1976).

Wa Thiongo Ngugi and Wa Mirii, Ngugi. *I Will Marry When I Want* (London: Heinemann, 1982).

# CHAPTER 3

# LOOKING BACK/LOOKING FORWARD: IDENTITY AND MEMORY IN AFRICAN FICTIONS OF EXILE [1]

In his seminal introduction to *The African Diaspora: African Origins and New World Identities*, [2] Isidore Okpewho identifies two very broad tendencies in discourses on diasporic identity. The first tendency, described as "Afrocentrist" is, according to the Nigerian scholar, characterized in general terms by a sense of origin and a continuous identification with Africa as a kind of homeland. Briefly but meticulously, Okpewho identifies various stages of the movement, starting from the time when the slaves first arrived the "New World," when all they had to cushion the crushing effects of the intolerable brutalities of the sugar-cane plantation was the memory of home, tracing it to Molefi Asante, the founder of Afrocentricity in its contemporary form, who articulates it as, and as Okpewho finally submits, "an institutionalization of a commitment that Black revolutionary leaders before him have had to make as they rallied their people around their beleaguered fate as a race." [3]

The second broad tendency is described as "Atlanticist" and refers generally to a position which denies any form of continuing relationship between the black people located in the West and those in the homeland of Africa. The argument simply is that too much water has passed under the bridge of time to make any such link still possible. It is clear that Gilroy's book,*The Black Atlantic: Modernity and Double Consciousness*, [4] supplies the term with which Okpewho captures the tendency. The part Caribbean, part black British scholar also represents the foremost representative of the tendency. His specific contribution lies in his conception of identity in trans-national terms. Gilroy is anti-race, anti-nation and anti-home, in

---

1 An earlier version of this chapter was first published in*Africa, Europe and (Post)Colonialism: Racism, Migration and Diaspora* (eds.) Susan Arndt & Marek von Brisinski. (Bayreuth: Bayreuth African Studies Series, 2006): 279 – 294

2 Isidore Okpewho, Carole Boyce Davies, & Ali A. Mazrui, ed., *The African Diaspora: African Origins and New World Identities* (Indiana: Indiana University Press, (2001).

3 Okpewho, Davies & Mazrui, African Diaspora, xvi.

4 Paul Gilroy, *The Black Atlantic: Modernity and Double Consciousness* (Cambridge, MA: Harvard University, 1993).

the natal sense. He defines the cultures of black people located in the West as traveling cultures. He celebrates Western modernity without any form of qualification and turns his back totally against what he terms as the "pre-rational" mode of traditional African thought.

As can be seen from the rough summary of the paradigms with which Okpewho classifies the contributions to the book, *The African Diaspora* focuses mainly on the cultural representations of the descendants of black people carried to the New world during the period of the trans-Atlantic slave trade. The six hundred-page book however devotes a few chapters to contemporary black migrants in Europe and America. Following Elabor- Idemudia, Okpewho describes this relatively fresh development as the "new African diasporas" arguing that what distinguishes them from what may now be referred to as the traditional diasporas lies in the circumstances under which they set sail from their homelands and which "qualify their relations with American society and their general sense of belonging, especially since they still have social and cultural roots back in their original homelands." [5]

This second category represents the focus of this chapter. The development, indeed, has, of recent, assumed some prominence in discourses of African cultural identity. This is because, and for reasons ranging from palpable material poverty, lack of intellectual and/or professional fulfillment and to political persecution, violent disturbances and war, several people from different African countries including writers, scholars, intellectuals and other cultural workers have continued to relocate from their home bases to different countries of Europe and America. Inevitably- or so it would seem – some of the writers affected are already reacting to this condition of displacement and loss in their works. They have been exploring the possibility of negotiating the gulf separating the homeland from an exile location. It is my intention in this chapter to propose a paradigm of articulating the transformation of exile and migration in African fiction. I illustrate the paradigm with an analysis of Dambudzo Marechera's collection of short stories *The House of Hunger.* [6]

## I: THEORISING DIASPORA

As is evident in my summary of Okpewho's introduction to *The African Diaspora,* two extreme positions are underlined in diasporic identity. On the one hand is a position suggesting that the black people living on the African continent have exactly the same identity genotype as those of the same complexion living in the Americas and in the countries of Europe. On the other hand is a position which re-

5 Okpewho, Davies, & Mazrui, *African Diaspora*, xxiv

6 Dambudzo Marechera, *A House of Hunger: Short Stories* (Oxford: Heinemann, 1993)

fuses to recognize any trace of Africanness in the being of these same people. My own question is: where in this paradigm does the African of the New Diasporas belong? Is identity simply a matter of here or there? What kinds of assumptions underline the variety of middle grounds implied in Okpewho's introduction? How, in short, do we conceive diasporic identity?

In approaching this question, I am assisted by Stuart Hall, the Jamaican-born black British cultural theorist who proposes two different perspectives of identity in his article "Cultural Identity and Diaspora." In the first perspective, identity is articulated as fixed, timeless and immutable. It is indeed seen as a finished product, already tightly packaged, and which is therefore unaffected by the vicissitudes of time and history. "Within the terms of this definition", I quote Stuart Hall:

> Our cultural identities reflect the common historical experiences and shared cultural codes, which provide us, as "one people", with stable, unchanging and continuous frames of reference and meaning, beneath the shifting divisions and vicissitudes of our actual history.[7]

This conception of identity constructs rigid boundaries between peoples, between ethnic groups, between nationalities and between races. Different identities do not flow into each other, or influence one another. Rather, they each maintain their places as well as their positions. Michael J.C Echeruo gestures toward this tendency in "An African Diaspora: the Ontological Project", an article which represents his contribution to *The African Diaspora*, the same book as I have earlier referred to. In his withering attack on Paul Gilroy, Echeruo states unequivocally in the article that identity is a state of being, an ontological project, in which it is impossible *not* to belong. He rails against the" indecent haste" with which certain black spokespersons rush to create new identities for black people. Using the actual words of Mary Robinson, the former Irish President, who in an address to the parliament in 1995 speaks glowingly of Irish identity both at home and in the diasporas, Echeruo argues that "a diaspora is a 'nation in exile,' a 'race in exile,' and a 'people in exile,'" and this, no matter how blurred the perspective of the word "exile" is, and no matter "how long it lasts and can last."[8]

Clearly, to Echeruo, identity is not a matter of choice, it is a matter of what you are and, as he further asserts, those who have a problem accepting the situation had better understand that "their options in the matter are very limited indeed. Put bluntly, they have none."[9] Gilroy, as Echeruo implies then, should simply face the

---

7 Stuart Hall, "Cultural Identity and Diaspora," in *Identity and Difference*, ed. Kathryn Woodward (London: SAGE, 1997): 51.

8 M.J.C. Echeruo, "An African Diaspora: The Ontological Project," in African Diaspora, ed. Okpewho, Davies, Mazrui, 8.

9 Echeruo, "An African Diaspora: The Ontological Project," 11

fact: as a black man, he is an African, an African who only happens to have been located in the West. And no matter how hard he tries; he will never be able to escape the fate.

Paul Gilroy certainly deserves to be tackled pointedly. And one gets the impression that Echeruo has deliberately adopted the polemical approach that is very obvious in the article precisely because of this purpose. There indeed are moments when he seems to be aware that things may not be so clear-cut. There are times when he demonstrates the knowledge that the concept of identity may not be so rigid, that it may not be so monolithic. When considered however in the context of the general thrust of the paper, these gestures appear muted and suppressed.

This leads me to the second perspective of identity as articulated by Stuart Hall. This second perspective acknowledges the influence of history and events in the shaping and re-shaping of identity. It questions the concept of *sameness* even as it does that of *fixedness* in identity constructions. Identities may be markedly similar but they will at the same time be markedly different. Different matrices of identity influence each other, but they are also affected by ruptures, accidents and discontinuities. Stuart Hall continues:

> Cultural identity, in this second sense, is a matter of "becoming" as well as of "being". It belongs to the future as much as to the past. It is not something which already exists, transcending place, time, history and culture. Cultural identities come from somewhere, have histories. But, like everything which is historical, they undergo constant transformation. Far from being eternally fixed in some essentialized past, they are subject to the continuous 'play' of history, culture and power. Far from being grounded in a mere 'recovery' of the past, which is waiting to be found, and which, when found, will secure our sense of ourselves into eternity, identities are the names we give to the different ways we are positioned by, and position ourselves within, the narratives of the past. [10]

As is clear from the quotation, the distinguishing factor in this second conception of identity inheres in the crucial role it assigns to history. It is certainly possible to speak about blackness or about Africanness. The problem, however, is that it will not take us too far. And soon, we will find ourselves returning to investigate the many tricks that history has played on either or both of the terms.

Hall himself exemplifies his thesis with black Caribbean identity insisting that its construction rests on two poles; with the first being that of "similarity" and "continuity" and the second that of "difference" and "rupture." Because it ensures a relationship with the past, the pole of similarity and continuity constantly reminds a typical Caribbean of his manner of his arrival at his/her present location. Yes, with arms and feet shackled, the original ancestors of black Caribbeans were "dragged" against their will into the ship and then transported into the New

[10] Hall, "Cultural Identity and Diaspora," 52

World. Prevented literally from taking any other thing along, all that these people had with them were their memories: memories of their different families, their different communities, and their different villages and traditions; memories, indeed, of the different languages they spoke and of the gods they worshipped. Fragments of these have continued to survive even till date. The gods for example live on, as Stuart hall tells us, "in the hybridized religious universe of Haitian voodoo, pocomania, native Pentecostalism, Black baptism, Rastafarianism and the black saints of Latin American Catholicism." [11]

The second pole, on the other hand, emphasizes the "broken" nature of this continuity. Even before their departures from Africa, differences existed among the slaves. They belonged to different cultures and societies for example, spoke different languages and practised different religions. They were also of different sexes and age grades. The moment the ships set sail from the African coast, these differences became blurred, and the links that the individual slaves had with their roots became simultaneously yet ruthlessly severed. In place of their traditional gods, the slaves were offered Christianity, while in place of their languages; they discovered that they had to adjust their tongues to either – depending on the specific location of their exiles – English, French, Portuguese or Spanish. In the plantation economy in which they now found themselves trying to grapple with their losses, the slaves discovered that they were soon to be joined by indentured labourers from India and China.

The memory of their different locations of departure remained but it was a memory that was already broken and which was no longer the same: the vision of home became more and more blurred with the passage of time. It was a vision on which history was to impact fundamentally. Africa continues to exist in the Caribbean but it is an Africa that has become totally different. It is an Africa that has been translated into a different language, an Africa that Benedict Anderson would have described as an "imagined community." [12]

> Everyone in the Caribbean, of whatever ethnic background, must sooner or later come to terms with this African presence. Black, brown, mulatto, white – all must look *Presence Africaine* in the face, speak its name. But whether it is, in this sense, an *origin* of our identities, unchanged by four hundred years of displacement, dismemberment, transportation, to which we could in any final or literal sense return, is more open to doubt. The original 'Africa' is no longer there. It too has been transformed. [13]

---

[11] Hall, "Cultural Identity and Diaspora," 53

[12] See Benedict Anderson, *Imagined Community: Reflections on the Rise and Spread of Nationalism* (London: Verso, 1983)

[13] Hall, "Cultural Identity and Diaspora," 55

## II: AFRICAN IDENTITIES IN THE DIASPORA

I agree fundamentally with Stuart Hall but because his example is drawn from the Black Carribean, I think I must at this point part ways with him. To make it clear, the specific point of difference between African and Caribbean identities lies in their relationship with Africa. Indeed, for the former, the homeland is real, palpable; it is not an imagined community. It is a concrete experience, a lived reality, encountered on a day – to – day basis. The experience is not homogeneous either. It is, on the contrary, diverse and multifarious. In his *Scars of Conquest/Masks of Resistance* Tejumola Olaniyan demonstrates great sensitivity to the multi-dimensional nature of African identities and realities. To be sure, Olaniyan's analysis benefits also from the works of Stuart Hall, even as it does from those of Paulin Hountodji [14] and Laclau and Mouffe. [15] The precise point of the book is its conception of identity in "performative terms." Olaniyan indeed proposes identity as a dynamic, open process, one that is forever being negotiated. Borrowing the word of Stuart Hall, the Nigerian scholar of African Studies defines culture as "articulation"; projecting it as a complex construction, the parts of which are structured together in different relationships of similarities and oppositions. The constituent elements of identity are not of equal value; rather they are structured in different degrees of "dominance and subordination." Writes Tejumola Olaniyan:

> The parts dominant in the articulated structure constitute what is commonly regarded as a people's distinct "way of life" at a given time. This distinctiveness has a historical character, and it is constantly being refashioned and reconstituted, for it is the site, and also the stake, of most often bitter social struggles. Culture here is perceived as a complicated strategic articulation of diverse and mutually contradictory elements or parts. In fact, the authority and necessity of articulation derive from the fact of cultures as composite of structures, and even its constitutive articulated parts or features are never immutable. [16]

Olaniyan's words are self explanatory and there is hardly a need to attempt any further explanation. Suffice it to emphasize the point that it is the dominant aspect of a tradition that distinguishes it from another one and that these distinguishing features themselves are historical in character. The dominant aspects of a culture represent the site of a constant battle as these elements are challenged by the contingent elements from within and by the foreign elements from without. Just as

---

14 See Paulin Hountondji, *African Philosophy: Myth and Reality* (London: Hutchinson University Library of Africa, 1983)

15 See Ernesto Laclau & Chantal Mouffe, *Hegemony and Socialist Strategy: Towards a Radical Democratic Politics* (London: Verso, 1985)

16 Tejumola Olaniyan, *Scars of Conquest/Masks of Resistance: The Invention of Cultural Identities in African, African – - American, and Caribbean Drama* (New York: Oxford UP, 1995): 36

cultural identity is not permanent so is it not autonomous or independent. Every culture exists in relation to other cultures and interacts with other traditions. Every identity is mutually imbricated with other identities. The word "foreign" which I employ above therefore applies to the new elements that are constantly being introduced into an identity. Together with the still surviving contingent elements, the new elements continue to assault the privileged elements within the dominant category or what Olaniyan would call the "historically expedient rallying point." [17] The result thus is a situation of permanent rancour. "The performative", says Olaniyan, "is the principle of a transgressive and transitional truth." [18]

The articulated elements constituting the characters of contemporary African traditions have undergone several transformations in recent time. It has, indeed, passed through several historical phases: it has passed "from the savage plunder of slavery and the slave trade", as Osundare puts it, "to the dispossession of colonialism, and ... (then) to the remote control stratagems of neo-colonialism." [19] What this means then is that, even before setting out, the subject of our discourse is, up to a point, already hybrid. S/he already has some prior engagement with the identity s/he has set out to encounter.

But while the above is true, it is also very important to qualify this engagement: it is indeed an absolute necessity to make what is obvious even clearer by stating that the engagement is not equal and that the other side has the upper hand. So before setting out, our exile, the African exile, occupies a position of disadvantage. S/he is, if somewhat bending the expression of Jacques Rabemananjara a little, a stealer of space. [20] Most likely, Nuruddin Farah would have put it differently. In *Yesterday, Tomorrow: Voices from the Somali Diaspora,* the book which records the experiences of those displaced in the Somali crisis, Farah, himself a migrant writer, writes of how, at a particularly distraught moment, he "understood the deeper meaning of a Somali wisdom in which a high value is placed on owning one's own home, as this affords an individual a greater sense of privacy, of self-honour and of dignity." [21] The exile then is a transgressor. Barehanded, s/he tries to dare the beast in its own cave.

---

17 Olaniyan, *Scars of Conquest*, 36

18 Olaniyan, *Scars of Conquest,* 36

19 Niyi Osundare, *Thread in the Loom: Essays on African Literature and Culture* (Trenton, NJ: Africa World Press, 2002): 139.

20 Jacques Rabemanannjara, at a 1956 Congress organised by Presence Africaine, describes colonised writers as "stealers of language." See Abiola Irele, "Second Language Literatures: an African Perspective," in *Thresholds: Anglophone African Literatures*, ed. Christiane Fioupou (Toulouse: Presses Universitaires du Mirail, 2000): 15

21 Nuruddin Farah, *Yesterday, Tomorrow: Voices from the Somali Diaspora* (Cassell: London, 2000): vii

Wole Soyinka captures the situation a little differently. He on his own describes exile as a "frontier of reality", as a "threshold" of ambiguity. [22] Osundare wrestles with the latter term, defining it as "the locus of indeterminacy and decision." When the poet in him takes over, what we have is a flow of clashing metaphors. The threshold, he says, is:

> Point and perimeter, sound and silence. It is both space, clamorous in its physicality and yet so affecting in its telluric silence. It is a grey zone whose tone is deeper than other colors. Like the bridge that it is, it looks forward by looking back, it looks back by looking forward. [23]

The threshold of exile is then a zone of trepidation. The subject faces two places at the same time. On the one hand is the memory of home and, on the other, the agonies of desolation. A disapora exists then in a halfway house, living as s/he does, in-between worlds, in-between cultures and in-between locations. In the rest of this chapter, I devote attention to the transformation of cultural identity in three short stories of Dambudzo Marechera. Since my interest lies directly in the exploration of movement of identity, it goes without saying that my preference is for that perspective which represents cultural tradition not as a fixed, stable category but rather, as one characterized by continuous diversification and self-renewal.

## III: THE HOUSE OF HUNGER

Marechera confesses to having found *The House of Hunger* as a difficult book to write. [24] At the time of writing it in 1976, the young author was in a crisis having just been expelled from the University of Oxford. With no fixed abode of his own, Marechera was, at the time, literally, and to use the words of Flora Veit Wild, his most authoritative scholar, a "homeless wanderer." [25] In an interview with Alle Lambu, which is included in Veit-Wild's *Dambudzo Marechera: a Source Book on his Life and Work*, Marechera makes it clear that his feeling at the time was that of total loss, of utter despair. Says he, inter-alia in the interview:

> Those of us who had gone to England or to any other country away from Ian Smith were expected to get degrees. We were of ourselves, and, after Independence, to return here with total dignity and respect. And here I was, having been expelled once again from Oxford and doing nothing at all except writing and drinking. That's when the exiled

22 Wole Soyinka, "Exile: Thresholds of Loss and Identity" in Fioupou, *Thresholds: Anglophone African Literatures*, 64

23 Osundare, *Thread in the Loom: Essays on African Literature and Culture*, 139

24 For details of Marechera's crisis during this period, see Flora Veit-Wild, *Dambudzo Marechera: A Source Book on his Life and Works* (London: Hans Zell, 1992): 151—183.

25 Veit-Wild,*Dambudzo Marechera: A Source Book on his Life and Works*, 176

Zimbabwean community started moving away from me and even beating me up, simply saying, "Dambudzo, you are a bad example, you have destroyed your whole educational prospects and you are giving Zimbabweans a bad image. [26]

Marechera really had a difficult time in Oxford. The picture that comes through from Veit-Wild's account is that of an over-sensitive young man who had carried his past on his shoulders. He had earlier been sent away from the University of Rhodesia having participated in students' protests against racial discriminations. Marechera was one person who never stooped because of anything. He was known to have betrayed intense hatred for his mother and sister who indulged in prostitution in order to make ends meet. He arrived in Oxford with a deep sense of humiliation and anger. His feeling of inferiority complex made him over-react to every issue, to every act of condescension – real and perceived – from members of his host society and even from fellow blacks from other African countries who generally affected some air of superiority before Zimbabweans.

Marechera just could not fit in, in short; and he never made any effort to do so. He violated all college rules and regulations and had violent clashes with several people. He indulged in excessive drinking and was arrested several times by the police for drunkenness. The situation reached a head, according to Veit-Wild, when "he assaulted students and members of the domestic staff, threatened to murder named people and to set the college on fire". [27] It was at this point that the college authority asked him to undergo psychiatric examination as a condition for his continued stay in the college. He still would not behave even after the doctors had given him a clean bill and the university authority in the end had no choice but to send him packing.

One other contradiction in Marechera's life, which Veit-Wild underlines in her book, is very important. Yes, Marechera intensely resented his host society yet he never wanted to leave it. Thus, while he felt deeply insulted by the suggestion that he had mental problems, he nonetheless consented to undergoing the test because of the fear that he might be forced to return to Zimbabwe. And even after he had been expelled, Marechera would rather opt for the life of a wanderer than travel back home. In terms of identity therefore, Marechera suffered from a deep crisis. Even though he behaved like an outsider, he was not ready to stay out. He therefore existed in a kind of limbo, that territory of exile, which Soyinka has characterized as the "threshold of loss." [28]

*The House of Hunger* is a work, which both captures this mood and offers an explanation for the crisis. The title story is autobiographical and represents a

---

[26] Veit-Wild, *Dambudzo Marechera: A Source Book on his Life and Works*, 25

[27] Veit-Wild,*Dambudzo Marechera: A Source Book on his Life and Works*, 159

[28] Wole Soyinka, "Exile: Threshold of Loss and Identity," 64

kind of reminiscence. The narrative is loose and long – winding. In its disordered and disjointed form, it reflects both the state of the mind of the narrator and the chaotic nature of the experience it projects. The "House of Hunger "serves as the dominant metaphor and it represents the identity background of the protagonist. The narration as I have said is autobiographical and it more or less projects Marechera trying to take a backward glance. The story is set in a colonized society, a racially segregated one for that matter. The narrator is a young man, a black man, an African. He is a member of the race who, in spite of being in the majority, has been relegated to the periphery. This young man has a very poor background and his parents can hardly make ends meet. The time setting reveals a moment of great historical ferment, a moment when people have risen up in protest against domination. The narrator is caught up in this crisis, even if in spite of himself and the reader encounters him being battered and badgered at different points in the story.

When the story opens, the protagonist is trying to escape from this house of hunger. Finding he has nowhere to go, he heads for a drinking joint. And no sooner had he settled down to a drink than he finds himself catapulted back to his past.

The "House of Hunger" is represented at multiple levels but all of them are characterized by violence, chaos and alienation. The narrator's family stands as the first and its defining hallmarks are a total absence of love, palpable poverty and incessant quarrels. Adults perpetrate acts of aggression against children. They are also unabashed in committing acts of sexual immorality. The narrator claims that it "was the House of Hunger that first made me discontented with things."

> I knew my father only as the character who occasionally screwed mother and who paid the rent, beat me up, and was cuckolded on the sly by various persons. He drove huge cargo lorries, transporting groundnut oil to Zambia and Zaire and Malawi. I knew that he was despised because of mother, and because he always wore khaki overalls, even on Sundays, and because he was quite generous with money to friends and enemies alike. The only thing was that he was an alcoholic. [29]

The mother in turn is described as a "hard worker in screwing, running a home, and maintaining a seemingly tight rein over her husband." [30] She is also presented as a great fighter, one who is very good at "verbal sallies" [31] and who never loses face. The other important person in the family is Peter, the narrator's elder brother. He is described as "the enemy of all fathers and mothers who had daughters."

---

[29] Dambudzo Marechera, *The House of Hunger*, 77
[30] Dambudzo Marechera, *The House of Hunger*, 78
[31] Dambudzo Marechera, *The House of Hunger*, 78

Both he and mother are said to have given to the "House a whiff of scandal strong enough to be detected throughout the whole region." [32]

The narrator's crisis deepens in school, which is the second level of representation of the House of Hunger. He is restless and thirsty for knowledge, like most of his contemporaries. He reads whatever comes his way apart, as he puts it, "from those which had been banned." [33] Involvement in politics and protests leads to arrests and brutalization and is to lead later, to his expulsion from the university. Acts of brutalities against each other are also not uncommon and the narrator takes time to report the clash between Stephen, the bully and Edmund, the poor, frail withdrawn boy who is later to become a guerrilla fighter.

And it is also during this period that the narrator undergoes a profound experience of hallucination. Here, at some length, is the way he captures the experience:

> It seemed to me something was taking over my body; the images and symbols I had for so long taken for granted had taken upon themselves a strange hue; and I was losing grasp of simple speech. I began to ramble, incoherently, in a disconnected manner. I was being severed from my own voice. I would listen to it as to a still, small voice coming from the huge distances of the mind. It was like this: English is my second language, Shona my first. When I talked it was in the form of an interminable argument, one side of which was always expressed in English and the other side always in Shona. At the same time I would be aware of myself as something indistinct but separate from both cultures. I felt gagged by this absurd contest between Shona and English. [34]

Could it mean then that the hallucination has been engendered by a complex crisis of identity? The young narrator seems unprepared for the contradictory forces kicking him from different sides and the inevitable result is psychological torture.

Of course, the larger society, which is the third level of representation of the metaphor of House of Hunger, stands as the ultimate generator of the whole crisis. As a victim, in many senses, of the violence and counter-violence of his racially structured society, the response of the narrator is that of estrangement, of ambivalence. While he loathes colonialism, he also projects an attitude of disidentification with expressions of nationalism. He refers to black heroism with cynicism throughout the story and does not hesitate to describe the word Zimbabwe inscribed on Julia's T-shirt as a "legend." [35] Marechera is not a person to accept such uncomplicated articulation of identity as proposed by Echeruo's ontological project. "No, I don't hate being black," says his protagonist later in the

[32] Dambudzo Marechera, *The House of Hunger*, 78
[33] Dambudzo Marechera, *The House of Hunger*, 2
[34] Dambudzo Marechera, *The House of Hunger*, 30
[35] Dambudzo Marechera, *The House of Hunger*, 19

story. "I'm just tired of saying it's beautiful. No, I don't hate myself. I'm just tired of people bruising their knuckles on my jaw." [36]

The obvious intention of this story is to enable the writer to retrace his steps to the point of beginning. As has been demonstrated, the picture painted by the protagonist of his background is not romantic, and it is indeed clear that his current problem has a long history. As the two cited passages indicate, a crisis of response is generated within the narrator by the two cultures kicking him from opposite sides. Ultimately, his attitude is not to identify with one or the other, but rather to see "myself as something indistinct but separate from both cultures." [37] This attitude of disavowal, especially toward his indigenous heritage, is an issue which marks the protagonist out in a number of significant ways.

## IV: IDENTITY AND THE PAST

This then is the story, which frames the narrator's background. The protagonist returns to it mainly for the purpose of self-apprehension. His articulated identity, by way of summary, is as a young African from a society that is still under colonial oppression. And there seems to be no escape from this history. Yet, is this really so? "Cultural identities come from somewhere, have histories," [38] says Stuart Hall. They also have courses, even if unstable. In "Black Skin, what Mask," we encounter another narrator who shares several things in common with the one in the title story. Like the one in "The House of Hunger," the protagonist is black, an African. He is from Zimbabwe. Unlike the protagonist in "The House of Hunger" however, his own location is Britain. Actually, he is a student in Oxford, a highly prestigious British institution.

In the context of the current story, and by virtue of his physical location however, this character constitutes a terrible minority. Unlike in the first story, there is no Harry, and no Phillips, no Stephen, no Julia and no Peter. None of those friends with whom he could indulge in scrapes. The trick which history has now played on him has ensured that he can only encounter white faces most of the time. It has also ensured that the few black faces that he will sometimes meet will not often be from Zimbabwe. Rather, they will be from West Indies or some such places or from Nigeria or any of the other so-called independent African countries. And because they come from countries that have already attained independence, these other Africans will most likely regard the protagonist with condescension. "My skin sticks out a mile in all the crowds around here." Says the narrator at the opening of the story:

---

36 Marechera, *The House of Hunger*, 45

37 Marechera, *House of Hunger*, 30.

38 Hall, "Cultural Identity and Diaspora," 52

> Every time I go out I feel it tensing up, hardening, torturing itself. It only relaxes when I am in shadow, when I am alone, when I wake up early in the morning, when I am doing mechanical actions, and, strangely enough, when I am angry. But it is coy and self-conscious when I draw in my chair and begin to write.
>
> It is like a silent friend: moody, assertive, possessive, callous – sometimes.[39]

There is only one other student who, being from Zimbabwe, the narrator shares almost totally the same identity with. Unlike however the protagonist who has taken a decision to deliberately exclude himself, this compatriot of his is prepared to go to any length in order to get accepted.

The story is much shorter than "The House of Hunger," and also less complex and convoluted. It is in fact simple and straight-forward, presented, as it were, from the viewpoint of the narrator and with the other character invited now and again, using the flashback technique, that is, to participate in a dialogue with the narrator. By this, the reader is able to listen, first hand, to each of the two compatriots' attitude to a condition of marginalization. Even though he is black, this other character is certainly ready to don a white mask. Some of the possibilities contemplated by him include scrubbing off his skin, getting rid of his accent, turning out in expensive attires and avoiding any Africans who would not conform to his own standard of proper conduct. But what does he get for all his efforts? Consistent rebuffs, pure and simple. It is not surprising to learn that having become eventually frustrated, he ends up slashing his own wrist and being taken to a "lunatic asylum."[40]

The narrator's own way of coming to terms with loneliness and rejection includes, on the other hand, alcoholism and violence. It is discovered presently that he himself has been asked to either submit himself for psychiatric examination or be expelled from the university. In a deliberate inversion of the details of an actual incident in the author's life, which has been briefly discussed earlier, the narrator in the story chooses to be sent down from the university. Asked by his friend if he would return home to participate in the liberation struggle, our protagonist demurs. Apparently for him, the options are not so clear-cut.

Tejumola Olaniyan describes identity as a "composite of structures,"[41] the constituent parts of which are never sacrosanct. Paulin Hountodji views it as an open set of options, [...] which by adopting one choice sacrifices all the others."[42] Admittedly, the dominant aspect of the protagonist's identity in "Black Skin, What Mask" may have been framed by his background in Zimbabwe, his stay in Oxford

---

39 Marechera, *The House of Hunger*, 93

40 Marechera, *The House of Hunger*, 93

41 Olaniyan, *Scars of Conquests*, 36

42 Paulin Hountodji, *Africa Philosophy: Myth and Reality,* 161

has, however, opened him up to new possibilities. Staying back in England to pursue a career in writing represents one of such possibilities and this is what he has opted for.

Again, the central character in "Thought – tracks in the Snow," the last story to be considered in this chapter is very close to his counterpart in "Black Skin, What Mask." Both of them are writers, and the two are also from Zimbabwe.

The hero in "Thought – tracks in the Snow" is in crisis. His career is in a mess and his marriage is also in trouble. The narrator takes stock of his past and present in the story. The mood therefore is sober. A brief reminiscence on his life in Africa brings him very close to the kind of situation witnessed in "The House of Hunger." It reminds him simply of tear gas fumes, police dogs, howling sirens. Fellow students are arrested en masse and carted into detention. White students stand by, meanwhile, applauding. Thought-tracks in the snow...

The manner of the protagonist's departure from homeland is also re-visited. It was a rushed exit, from all indications, one, which, in the hurry of it all, he even forgot to take his spectacles with him. So, sitting in the plane, sipping whisky, the narrator wonders whether there is anything else that he has left behind:

> Who was I leaving behind? My own prematurely grey head still sat stubbornly upon my shoulders; my family did not know where I was or whether I was alive or dead. I do not think that they would have cared one way or the other had they known that at that moment I was thousands of feet above the earth, hanging as it were in the emptiness which my dabbling with politics created for me. I felt sick with everything, sick with the self-pity, sick with the Rhodesian crisis, sick! [43]

Clearly, the protagonist suffers from a profound experience of alienation. He is alienated from his family. He is alienated also from his country. He is totally alienated, in short, from his past. And, as the story demonstrates, he is not in any hurry to reconcile with it.

But what then is his choice? What option has he negotiated for himself? In what direction is he headed? As the plane tears through the night, heading towards Oxford, the narrator claims he knows that "before me were years of desperate loneliness, and the whisky would be followed by other whiskies, other self-destructive poisons..." [44]

[43] Marechera, *The House of Hunger*, 144

[44] Marechera, *The House of Hunger*, 143–44

## V: CONCLUSION

One thing that seems common to the three stories isolated for investigation in this essay are the feelings of almost total lack of identification with the homeland on the part of their respective protagonists. A factor, however, that seems to somewhat counter – balance this position lies in the attitude of overwhelming rejection of their exile condition by the same characters. In the first story, the main character sets out determined to escape from what he has described as the "House of Hunger," only to discover that he has nowhere to go. The second story is set in exile and the student protagonist has difficulties adjusting to his new environment. When he is asked, however, whether he would like to return to Africa, his answer is firmly in the negative. The third and final story explains the incoherence in the present condition of the exile protagonist in terms of the crisis of the past. Yet, the impression the reader gets is that nothing is likely to be done about the situation. Taken together then, what we have in the three stories is the pathetic condition of exiles who seem trapped in mid – flight; who, to spell it out, are neither able to move forward nor undertake a return journey. In their permanent state of suspension therefore, the three protagonists can be seen in terms of what Soyinka has described as an Esu character in his "Threshold of Loss".

As the Yoruba god of chance and indeterminacy, Esu has a propensity for generating acrimony and rancour and it is for this reason that the deity is, according to Soyinka, never "welcome within the home" of the Yoruba people and why his shrine is always located "just outside the doorway, on the threshold of habitation." [45] Esu is a permanent wanderer and Marechera's characters, in their feelings of perpetual displacements and dislocations, seem to derive great inspiration from him. The three characters appear, indeed, to be at one with this god in their liminal existence.

As a final word, let me state that all exile characters articulate this feeling of complicated ambivalence toward both their original home and also their country of habitation. For them, the line separating the land of birth from a diasporic location is never easy to draw and hence, no simple identification can be possible. All they can do is to make the best of multiple cultural alternatives, appropriating them in their perpetual struggle for identity re-placements. At this point, one problem that must be identified with regards to Marechera's protagonists is that they tend – without exception and like Esu, their alter ego – toward the extremes. If, therefore, there is any difference between Marechera and other African writers of the diaspora such as Abdulrazak Gurnah, Buchi Emecheta, Ike Oguine and Cheikh Hamidou Kane, it would seem to lie in the way these other writers have managed to moderate their characters' articulation of their acute experience of

[45] Soyinka, "Exile", 67

displacement and dislocation. In the way these writers struggle to negotiate places of abode for their wandering heroines and heroes in their respective places of exile, even as they simultaneously set them apart from these societies. It may be stated, tentatively, that these other positions appear more productive as alternative representations of identity and memory in African fiction of the second diaspora.

## WORKS CITED

Anderson, Benedict. *Imagined Community: Reflections on the Rise and Spread of Nationalism* (London: Verso, 1983).

Echeruo, M.J.C. "An African Diaspora: the Ontological Project," in *The African Diaspora: African Origins and the New World Identities* ed. Isidore Okpewho, Carole

Boyce Davies & Ali A. Mazrui (Indiana: Indiana University, 2001): 3—18.

Farah, Nuruddin. *Yesterday, Tomorrow: Voices from the Somali Diaspora* (London: Cassell, 2000).

Gilroy, Paul. *The Black Atlantic: Modernity and Double Consciousness* (Cambridge, MA: Harvard University, 1993).

Hall, Stuart. "Cultural Identity and Diaspora," in *Identity and Difference*, ed. Kathryn Woodward (London: SAGE, 1997): 51—58.

Hountodji, Paulin. *African Philosophy: Myth and Reality* (London: Hutchinson University Library of Africa, 1983).

Irele, Abiola. "Second Language Literatures: an African perspective," in *Thresholds: Anglophone African Literatures*, ed. Christiane Fioupou (Toulouse: Presses Universitaires du Mirail, 2000): 7 – 22.

Laclau Ernesto & Chantal Mouffe. *Hegemony and Socialist Strategy: Towards a Radical Democratic Politics* (London: Verso, 1985).

Marechera, Dambudzo.*The House of Hunger: Short Stories* (Oxford: Heinemann, 1993).

Okpewho, Isidore. "Introduction," in *The African Diaspora: African Origins and New World Identities*, ed. Isidore Okpewho, Carole Boyce Davies & Ali A. Mazrui (Indiana: Indiana University, 2001) x–xxviii.

Olaniyan, Tejumola. *Scars of Conquest/Masks of Resistance: The Invention of Cultural Identities in African, African – American, and Caribbean Drama* (New York: Oxford UP, 1995).

Osundare, Niyi.*Thread in the Loom: Essays on African Literature and Culture* (Trenton, NJ: AWP, 2002).

Soyinka, Wole. "Exile: Thresholds of Loss and Identity," in *Thresholds: Anglophone African Literatures*, ed. Christiane Fioupou (Toulouse: Presses Universitaires du Mirail, 2000): 6–70.

Veit – Wild, Flora.*Dambudzo Marechera: A Source Book on His Life and Works* (London: Hans Zell, 1992).

# CHAPTER 4

# 'THE PRESENT POSITION ON THE PRESENT CONDITION OF THE PRESENT SITUATION': A STUDY OF KEN SARO – WIWA'S SELECTED FICTIVE WRITINGS [1]

Injustice stalks the land like a tiger on the prowl. [2]

We write best of the things we directly experience, better of what we hear, and well of what we imagine [3]

The title of this chapter has been so constructed, deliberately. It is an attempt at preserving the pattern of a written query addressed to Ken Saro-Wiwa by his father on the eve of Nigeria's civil war (1967 – 1970). The latter had been greatly disturbed by his son's implacable opposition to the concept of Biafra, even when the young man worked right among the core of secessionist intellectuals. So, in a letter written to him in Mid-June, 1967, the old Saro-Wiwa had asked his son rather tautologically: "With regard to the present condition of the present situation, what is your present position?" [4]

To be sure, Ken Saro-Wiwa has always insisted on a united Nigeria. He still reiterated this position in an interview with *The News*, a Nigerian news magazine in May, 1993. In what was to turn out to be one of his last engagements with the press, the late minority rights activist makes it clear that the aim of the agitation he championed was not to break away from Nigeria. In any event, as he adds by way of a light digression, he himself still had people whose company he cherished. It is interesting of course, that of the seven names he cited, six are

1 An earlier version of this chapter was first published in *Ken Saro – Wiwa and the Crises of the Nigerian State*, ed. Omotoye Olorode, Wumi Raji, Jiti Ogunye & Tunde Oladunjoye (Lagos: CDHR, 1998):193 – 207

2 Ken Saro – Wiwa, "We will defend our Oil with our Blood." Interview *Tell* (February 8, 1993): 28

3 Ken Saro – Wiwa, "They are Killing my People." Interview *The News* (May 17, 1993): 44

4 For further details on this, see Ken Saro-Wiwa, *On a Darkling Plain: An Account of the Nigerian Civil War* (Port Harcourt: Saros International Publishers, 1989): 90 – 91.

writers of great renown. [5] And Fela Anikulapo-Kuti, the seventh person, though not a writer, was also a great artist, a musician of immeasurable talent and an implacable scourge of the establishment. Never known to leave any matter hanging, the executed president of the Movement for the Survival of the Ogoni People (MOSOP) immediately adds that for the continued existence of the country to be possible, there must exist, a condition of social justice. [6]

The perspective articulated by Saro-Wiwa on the role of the writer in the struggle to achieve a just society is extremely engaging. In *A Month and a Day*, his detention diary published posthumously, Saro-Wiwa maintains that "literature in a critical situation such as Nigeria's cannot be divorced from politics" [7]. And being wedded to politics here goes beyond standing by the side to reflect on the society.

Such a position, according to him, can hardly be effective, since most people can neither read nor write while those who possess the requisite skills have "little time for the luxury of literary consumption beyond the need to pass examinations based on set texts". [8] Consequently then, and as Saro Wiwa insists, the writer must be a man of action, one who is practically involved in politics and who is actively engaged in mass organizations. Says he:

> He (the writer) must establish direct contact with the people and resort to the strength of African literature-oratory in the tongue. For the word is power and more powerful is it when expressed in common currency. That is why a writer who takes part in mass organizations will deliver his message more effectively than one who writes waiting for time to work its literary wonders. A struggle (of authenticity) will necessarily ensue, but that should conduce to making the writer even better. [9]

Saro-Wiwa claims to have derived this perspective from the examples of "the best" of Nigerian writers including, as he says, Wole Soyinka, the Nobel laureate, "the normally placid and wise Chinua Achebe", Christopher Okigbo who died fighting on the Biafran side during the civil war and Festus Iyayi who was dismissed as a lecturer from the University of Benin in the eighties due to his involvement in trade union struggles. [10] Saro – Wiwa himself, following the examples of the writers he had listed, had had to commit his awesome resources as a writer and publisher to the cause of his Ogoni homelands, a minority but oil-rich community

---

5 Precisely, the people mentioned are Wole Soyinka, Fela Anikulapo-Kuti, Kole Omotoso, Niyi Osundare, J.P. Clark, Elechi Amadi and Chinua Achebe. See "They Are Killing My People," 23.

6 "They are Killing my People," 23

7 Ken Saro – Wiwa, *A Month and a Day*. (London: Penguin, 1995): 81

8 *A Month and a Day*, 81

9 *A Month and a Day*, 81

10 *A Month and a Day*, 82

of about five hundred thousand people located in the North-Eastern part of the Niger-Delta, on the one hand, and the entire Nigerian community, on the other. Altogether, Saro-Wiwa has about sixteen published works of fiction including four novels, two volumes of short stories, a collection of Ogoni folktales, a collection of poetry, two volumes of plays and six children's books.

In this short, introductory chapter on his works, I undertake a close – up study of three of the texts, namely: *Sozaboy*, his very first novel, *A Forest of Flower*, a collection of short story; and *Basi and Company: Four Television Plays*, a collection of drama. In studying them, my aim is to articulate how these works simultaneously represent the basis, as well as an extension, of Saro Wiwa's practical involvement in the multi-dimensional politics of post-colonial Nigeria.

*Sozaboy*[11] a novel written in experimental English shares a lot in common with *On a Darkling Plain* 'Saro-Wiwa's diary dedicated to the Nigerian civil war. Though one is fictive, and the other autographical, both works are deliberately focused on the civil war that ravaged Nigeria between 1967 and 1970 and both of them articulated similar perspective of the incident. In both works, Saro Wiwa's statement is, directly, to the effect that the ethnic minorities of Eastern Nigeria were no more that mere pawns in what he sees as the Biafran secessionist gamble. Of course, Ogoni, his own indigenous group, a people for whom he has nurtured profound worry since childhood represents his foremost concern.

# I

Saro-Wiwa was a young academic at the University of Nigeria, Nsukka at the outbreak of hostility in 1967. First fleeing Nsukka for Bori, his home town, Saro-Wiwa had then hired a canoe, navigated his way through the maze of the Creeks of the Niger Delta, hitting the Atlantic at Bonny from where he eventually sailed to Lagos to declare his support for the Federal side. He was soon to become a member of the cabinet in-exile of the then newly created Rivers State, and when, soon after, the oil terminal of Bonny was captured by the Federal troops in November of the same year, Saro-Wiwa was appointed as the administrator of the strategically located coastal town. His assignment, which included that of re-settling the civilian population and assisting the Federal troops in penetrating the Biafran heartland, gave Saro-Wiwa the opportunity to observe the war from a very close and highly privileged position.[12] In *Sozaboy,* the author re-captures these first-hand experiences in fictive terms.

---

11 Ken Saro Wiwa, *Sozaboy: a Novel in Rotten English* (Port Harcourt: Saros International Publishers, 1985)

12 For further details on this, see *On a Darkling Plain* (Port Harcourt: Saros International Publishers, 1989)

The story is presented as an account of the war experiences of the people of Dukana, a community which features prominently in Saro-Wiwa's imaginative writings. From its description as a distinct, though small, riverine, community located on the fringe of Port Harcourt, it is not particularly difficult to establish a correspondence between it and the author's homeland of Ogoni. The story is presented partly as a quest, put forward as it were, as a first-hand experience of Sozaboy, the eponymous hero of the novel. It commences at the point when the war just breaks out and the reader watches the young hero as he abandons his wife and mother to join the army. At this point, he is all-enthusiasm – very naïve and stupid even. As he sees it, the military is nothing but fun, nothing but the uniform which makes a man to walk tall, erect and proud both in the company of his peers and among the people of his native community. Says he, in his primary school English, of the reasons why he wants to enlist in the army:

> I have determined to be Soza because one, Zaza is prouding and giving me assault because I am not Soza, and two, because the thick man says Dukana boys must join Soza that their own salt has salt inside it and three, because some girls who are making simple Defence are giving me moless on the way to Pitakwa and four, because Agnes my lover say I must join Soza and five, because of what the tall man was saying in the African Upwine Bar plus the fine fine uniform with badge which those young Sozas were wearing in the army camp plus how Chief Birabee is smiling foolish idiot smile whenever e see Zaza. [13]

This period of unqualified innocence is bound to be short-lived. Confronted by the havocs and horrors of war, Sozaboy shrinks. But as terribly ill-equipped as he is, he survives all dangers and disasters. Since Saro – Wiwa deliberately constructs him like a hero in a mythical narrative, he must live to recount the tale. He finds himself at different sides of the war at different points in time and is soon to engage in a gruelling search for his wife and mother. The search takes him first to Dukana which he discovers to have been sacked completely and which is now as "silent like church on Monday." [14] The grim picture of desolation is later intensified by the testimony of horror he receives from the two people he eventually finds in a nearby farm. And as he moves from one open camp to another, he receives further stories regarding the terrible experience of Dukana people: how they have been singled-out for special ill-treatment, how they have been starved and maimed and killed and fed upon and how even many, many more have been left to die of ill – health and kwashiorkor. They are considered as deserving of this experience directly because they have been accused of having deliberately allowed the enemy into Dukana and, ultimately Nugwa, the newly declared state. The story had better be presented in the words of Zaza, the world war veteran:

---

[13] *Sozaboy*, 59

[14] *Sozaboy*, 144

"when any of those big guns begin to shoot, we just look for the nearby bush or lorry just put head begin dey go until we no fit hear the noise of gun again. That is how we have been running since that first day of fight near Dukana. And as the guns dey chase us that day, na so dem dey chase us till today. When we hear the gun, we just run like goat or illama. We no care where we dey go just dey run like foolish idiots. Na so we run sotey we come reach this Nugwa where everybody is saying na we allow the enemy to come inside Dukana and now we are inviting the enemy to Nugwa. So all people do not want to see Dukana porson. When they ask you where you come from and you say you come from Dukana, then immediately they will ask you to leave their town. They will not give you food to eat, they will not give you water to drink, if you sick, nothing to cure you. Sozaboy, na for God hand we dey. True, true, I have seen them kill and eat some Dukana people."[15]

The fictive veil is very thin at this point. Very, very thin. Because, in *On a Darking Plain*, Saro-Wiwa has agonized deeply on what he describes as "the full effect of what it means to be an extreme minority in the society that is Nigeria."[16] Beyond that, he has written of how the Ogonis who found themselves as refugees in Biafra during the war were deliberately isolated for punishment.

According to his accounts, the Federal troops had very little difficulty in penetrating the Ogoni sector during the war. So terrible was the situation for the secessionists that many of the field commanders had to be court-martialed by Odumegwu Ojukwu, Head of State and Commander – in – Chief of the Armed Forces of the Republic of Biafra. The major defence put up by these helpless commanders had been to the effect that the Ogonis themselves had colluded with the enemy troops and had shown them routes hitherto unknown to the Biafran soldiers. The story was believed in its entirety and the Ogoni refugees were to pay dearly for it. Their experiences, if Saro – Wiwa's accounts are to be believed were very, very similar to what has been related above. This should make clear the full import of the second epigram with which this article has been opened which, of course, is only in line with Saro-Wiwa's articulated perspective of the role of the writer in the society.

*Sozaboy* closes on an ironic note. The hero takes substantial risks during the war trying to locate Dukana people. Now following the surrender of Nugwa army, these people relocate to their community. But Sozaboy cannot re-join them since he is believed to have died during the war. He is now seen as a ghost that has continued to haunt Dukana and its citizens, afflicting them with a disease which kills almost at the instant. The only way out, as they are to discover through a jujuman, is to capture this ghost and give it a proper burial. Sozaboy knows better than to take a risk with these extremely ignorant and superstitious people. He

---

15 *Sozaboy*, 145

16 *On a Darkling Plain*, 151

flees. And as he proceeds on exile, he ruminates on "how the war have spoiled my town Dukana, uselessed many people, killed many others, killed my mama and my wife... and now it have made me like porson wey get leprosy because I have no town again." [17]

*A Forest of Flowers* [18] is Saro-Wiwa's best-known book of short stories. With a total of nineteen stories, the collection is divided into two rough parts. The first part, containing eight stories and subtitled "Home, Sweet Home" is an involved depiction of rural, pristine existence. We meet the people of Dukana, this time in their natural rural environment, acting out their customs and traditions and without the threat of any war. The second part, on the other hand, is relatively more cosmopolitan, taking up, as it were, the varied themes of modernity, including, among others, highlife, crimes and the domestic dilemmas of the emergent middle-class women. In this essay, my focus is on the first part of the collection. My argument, directly, is that the eight stories presented therein articulate the author's conviction concerning the plight of his people and the underlying urgency for the emergence of an intellectual who will lead the people in a struggle against what is perceived as the dangers of complete annihilation.

Now, every one of the eight stories bears clear rings of irony. The involved narrator/persona has just completed her studies in the city and is returning home to take up a teaching appointment in the only primary school that the village, at present, can boast of. The little education she herself had received had been through sheer accident since, traditionally, most girls of her age grade are expected to stop their education even before the end of elementary six. Sira, her childhood friend represents a veritable example. Though brilliant, Sira had to stop going to school partly because her parents could not afford the fees and more importantly because being an only child, the responsibility had devolved upon her to raise children in order to keep on the name of the family. The ironic point in the story however lies in the grim condition of a people who are neglected and backward but who regard themselves with great pride and admiration.

As we are told in the title story of the part, Dukana lacks all facilities necessary for good and meaningful existence. These, bluntly put, include water, light, health-care facilities and good school. But, as virtually everyman and woman within the community believe, only malicious and ill-intentioned people would, because of this, conclude that the place is undeveloped. Such a person would be deserving of unqualified contempt and ridicule. After all, had Dukana:

> Not won wars against neighbouring kingdoms? Had she not preserved her independence from time immemorial? And did the people need anyone to feed them? Was there not

[17] *Sozaboy*, 181

[18] Ken Saro – Wiwa, *A Forest of Flowers* (Port Harcourt: Saros International Publishers, 1989)

peace? And did not people go about their daily chores in tranquillity? And if anyone thought Dukana was not progressive, what about the school they had established which had been duly approved by Government to present pupils for the elementary six certificate? And what of their lorry 'Progress' which was the only vehicular transport serving Dukana and her neighbours? [19]

So life goes on, even if it is simple and unexciting, and even if it is primitive and short. Daily, the people troop out of their mud houses covered with raffia palms, trudging to the forest to till the land and tend the crops or to the network of rivers and creeks to hunt for fishes and such other sea foods. In the evening, they return to the villages to listen to the embellished tales of tortoise handed down from ancient times or to the rhythms of drums welling up from the village square. They live on, in their dreams and fantasy, determined forever to avert anything that threatens those things to which they have become accustomed.

"The Inspector Calls" presents one of the methods by which these people execute their resistance against all plagues. Of course, the persona, because of her education and exposure, agrees that given the terribly filthy condition of the village, the services of a sanitary inspector is required. His visit, at least, will make the people attend to the overgrown grass in the village and the excrement of both children and domestic animals that litter all places.

But ancient wisdom holds differently. And so when the appointed day arrives, the spirit of the land simply "took over (the inspector's) motorcycle and led him to the house of the Chief where Birabee and his assembled assistants fed him with good things of life and gave him a good, fat envelope... and made sure he drank alcohol to his heart's delight and then led him out again, on the same path by which he had come." [20]

Ignorance, superstition and illiteracy constitute the real disease plaguing these people. In making this statement, I am reminded of the way *Sozaboy* ends and of the tragic plot of "The Bonfire".

Nedam, the major character in this latter story, is different from all the other young men in the village. Nedam keeps to himself, withdrawn and taciturn as he is. Not being able to understand him, the villagers decide on their own conclusion: he is a terribly wicked person, loaded to the teeth, as it were, "with things dangerous, things mysterious, things potent, things powerful and things supernatural." [21] He is, indeed, the cause of all untimely deaths in the village!

But Nedam, in actuality, stands as a positive potential to the community. With a large, well-cultivated and intelligently planned oil-palm plantation located deep

[19] *A Forest of Flowers*, 3
[20] *A Forest of Flowers*, 17
[21] *A Forest of Flowers*, 35

inside the forest, the young man has a gaze and a vision set well beyond Dukana. But he would not disclose this to anybody. As it would happen however, a citizen of Dukana resident in another part of the country and who, by the standard of the village is clearly doing well suddenly drops dead, far away in the city where he lives. "The autopsy conducted in far away Kano where Alee worked... spoke of diabetes. Dukana spoke of envy, magical spells, poisons, mumbo-jumbo and necromancy, all emanating from Dukana, of course." [22] This is Saro Wiwa, underlining in a very ironic way, the profound ignorance in which the people of Dukana wallow. Having identified Nedam as the person responsible for Alee's death, and determined to prevent him from perpetrating further atrocities, the youth of the village take a decision to get rid of him. They seize the young man, bind him hands and feet, lock him up in his hut and set the thatched contraption on fire. They disperse at the end of it all satisfied that they have rid the community of its only evil.

The persona suffers the most for all this. Her knowledge of other things and other places makes her awareness of the people's backwardness highly acute. She understands the speed with which the rest of humanity moves, out there, and she feels pained in her realization that as an oil-producing community, her village possesses the resources with which to undertake the race with the rest of the world. It is probably important to return, once more, to "Home, Sweet Home".

> I felt that excruciating pain which knowledge confers on those who can discern the gulf, which divides what is, and what could be. And my mind drifted to the men and women of Dukana acting out their lives against a backdrop of great forces they would never understand. I thought at length about them, the men and women whom I knew were awaiting my return because they were my relatives – aunts, uncles, cousins, my kin. And I felt for them [23]

There is no mistaking the tone of determination. The persona has decided to return, and to lead her people in the struggle to destroy the gulf that separates them from modernity. She stands as Saro-Wiwa's alter ego.

*Basi and Company: Four Television Plays* is a selection from 'Basi and Company,' the television series which Saro-Wiwa created and produced for the Nigerian Television Authority in the eighties. By far the most popular of all of Saro-Wiwa's creative efforts, *Basi and Company* is a situation comedy representing the author's attempt at influencing public morality in Nigeria. Woven around the well-worn theme of a greedy individual who wants to acquire great wealth without working for it, *Basi and Company* had, by its peak in 1986, an estimated thirty million viewers scattered all over the country.

[22] *A Forest of Flowers*, 38

[23] *A Forest of Flowers*, 5

There is no doubt that Saro-Wiwa committed himself fully to the project. Beside creating the series and crafting over sixty of the episodes, he also, at least going by his own admission, financed the production. Beyond this, the author has adapted the series in several other genres. It has been re-worked for "younger readers" in *The Adventures of Mr. B Series,* as prose-fiction for intermediate readership in *Mr. B* and *Mr. B Again*; and as a full-length novel in *Basi and Company: A Modern African Folktale*. All of them adopt the same quasi-farcical cum satirical mode, presenting the same characters, narrating the same story, and projecting the same theme of excessive love of wealth. It is certainly a measure of Saro-Wiwa's commitment to the moral health of Nigerian society that he could commit so much time, energy and resources to the project.

But perhaps the author has for long before it took off thought about the project. Because, by 1985 when it eventually commenced on the Nigerian Television, *The Transistor Radio* the first episode in the series, had existed for at least thirteen years. Presented also as number one in the printed text, *Four Television Plays*, "The Transistor Radio" won a BBC African Theatre prize in 1972.

Anyhow, the scene of the television serial is Adetola Street, a long, busy Lagos street, according to the dramatist; "noisy with a variety of houses and business concerns including churches, prayer houses and mosques" [24] The major characters are six in number. There is Basi himself, the man who comes to Lagos with the aim of making money but through anything other than honest means. Fondly called Mr. B, Basi leads a despicable existence. He spends all his time scheming and dreaming. The dreams fail all the time but Mr. B is not one to give up. There is Madam, Basi's vulgar landlady. She is as greedy for wealth as Basi, and is a person of loud manners and flambouyant appearance. Dandy is the middle-age owner of the bar on Adetola Street. Himself an alcoholic, Dandy's bar business is in ruins but his hope is to make it big in ways other than this particular enterprise. Alali lives with Basi at No 7, Adetola Street. Saro-Wiwa sketches the background of this particular character in *Mr. B,* the intermediate prose-fiction adaptation of the drama series. A secondary school graduate, Alali had come to Lagos in search of a job. But having walked the streets for several months without luck, he is left with no choice other than to rest his hope on Basi's schemes. Finally are Josco, a jail-breaker who takes refuge in Dandy's bar and Segi, a stereo-type of a city-girl, fun-loving and smashing in appearance. Saro-Wiwa writes of them all in "Guidelines to Basi and Company"

The characters all live on Adetola Street. Basi, Alali and Madam at No. 7 which belongs to

[24] Ken Saro – Wiwa "Basi and Company: Guidelines for Writers," Unpublished Mimeograph. Saro-Wiwa had to issue this guideline when it was becoming impossible for him to combine scripting the series with his other numerous assignments.

the latter. With the exception of Segi and to some extent, Josco, they all believe in making big money quickly. And are prepared to do anything to achieve that aim. The schemes their fertile imagination conjures up are sometimes as fantastic as they are sure to fail. Envy, hatred and petty jealousies are common among them, and they will often place blocks of stumble in each other's way just to ensure that not one of them succeeds[25].

*Basi and Company* is a searing indictment of Nigerian public life. As Saro-Wiwa himself says, all the characters are "common in Nigerian society", a society which has relegated honesty and hard-work to the background, enthroning falsehood and chicanery in its place. Everybody wants to get rich but nobody wants to work for it. So Basi and his colleagues continue to scheme but the moral preacher in Saro-Wiwa continues to ensure their failure. In *The Transistor Radio*, Josco and Dandy plan to do some fast business with Segi's radio. This, however, backfires and they lose the radio to the bargain. *Comrades All* resolves the crisis consequently generated. Segi recovers her radio, Alali, his one naira and Madam, her empty bottle of Saros lager. Everyone is happy. Everybody is a comrade. In *A Shipload of Rice,* Basi wins the sales contract of a consignment of rice being shipped in from America. Not possessing the capital required for such business however, Basi's simple plan is to transfer the contract to his landlady after having added five naira to the cost price of each of the 200,000 bags. Basi's hope of earning a "cool" million blows up in his face in the end as the contract papers are discovered to be fake. Basi in addition gets into trouble with Madam from whom he has already collected some money.

The above examples serve to demonstrate the story line of the drama which follows the pattern of conventional morality tale. Going back to *Mr. B,* we remember how Alali arrives in Lagos, carrying with him the lesson taught him by his father to the effect that only a person who works hard can make money. Saro-Wiwa upholds this elementary principle to the letter throughout the series ensuring that all efforts to violate it do not succeed.

It has been claimed that the audience of *Basi and Company* cuts across different classes in Nigeria.[26] But even if this is true, it may not be for the reason proposed by the reviewer of the series in *New York Times.*[27] As a witty, hilarious presentation, *Basi and Company* could represent a veritable opportunity for relax-

25 "Guidelines," 4

26 On the blurb of the published selection from the television series is an extract from a review in *South Magazine*, which claims that the production "is watched by a huge audience that cuts across all classes of Nigerian society". See Ken Saro-Wiwa, *Basi and Company: Four Television Plays*. (Port Harcourt: Saros International Publishers, 1989).

27 On the same blurb is another extract, this time from *New York Times*, claiming that Basi and Company seems to have struck a chord because it lampoons modern Nigeria's get rich quick mentality. See *Basi and Company,* blurb

ation for certain members of the upper and middle class especially after a hectic day of shouting, yelling and heckling in the offices, and at the factory. Added to this is the support it gives to the point that has always been drummed into the workers' head regarding the need to work hard for an "honest" pay.

A similar dimension could be discerned from Saro-Wiwa's ethnic formulation of the Nigerian problem; which formulation has hopefully been presented in the two texts earlier studied in this essay. There is no doubt, for sure, that the Ogoni people, nay the various ethnic minorities in Nigeria, experience untold deprivation and neglect. But to then insist, as Saro-Wiwa often does, that the forces conspiring against them are "the three old adversaries" [28] is at least, to indulge in gross generalization. It is, to express it differently, to confuse the interest of the common people with that of the elite. Like the Ogonis, majority of Yoruba people, of Hausa people and of Igbo people are also marginalized and neglected. They have no good jobs, no access to education, no health facilities and no functioning infrastructure. For Saro-Wiwa not to understand this is for his conception of the notion of justice to be somewhat flawed.

[28] By the "three old adversaries," Saro – Wiwa refers to the three major ethnic groups in Nigeria namely: the Hausa – Fulani, the Yorubas and the Igbos. As the late minority rights activist contends, these three groups had fought the war in order to be able to control "the oil wealth of our areas." See *On a Darkling Plain*, 238.

## WORKS CITED

Saro-Wiwa, Ken,*Basi and Company: Four Television Plays*. (Port Harcourt: Saros International Publishers, 1989).

– "Basi and Company: Guidelines for Writers" Unpublished Mimeograph.

– "Basi and Company: Elements of Plot" Unpublished Mimeograph.

– *On a Darkling Plain: An Account of the Nigerian Civil War* (Port Harcourt: Saros International Publishers, 1989)

– *A Forest of Flowers: Short Stories*. (Port Harcourt: Saros International Publishers, 1989)

– *A Month and a Day* (London: Penguins, 1995)

– "They Are Killing My People. Interview. (*The News*, May 17, 1993).

– "We will Defend our Oil with our Blood." Interview. *Tell* (February 8, 1993)

– *Sozaboy: A Novel in Rotten English* (Port Harcourt: Saros International Publishers, 1985)

# CHAPTER 5

# THEATRE, SOCIETY AND THE CHALLENGES OF AMATEUR PRODUCTION IN NIGERIA: A REVIEW CRITIQUE OF AKANJI NASIRU'S "LET'S FIND AN ANSWER"[1]

Till about the middle of the nineties, University of Ilorin happened to be, ironically, one of the few Universities in Nigeria that retained a relatively vibrant theatre culture. Ironically because, the University, as at the time, and even till now, had no standard theatre structure. The multi-purpose Africa Hall, which then functioned as lecture theatre, centre for religious worship and venue for social occasions, served also as the main theatre, complemented by the then Performing Arts courtyard. Indeed, such Nigerian Universities which, during the period, boasted of modern theatre buildings complete with up-to-date equipment and gadgets actually had much fewer performances.[2] This, in the main, was due to the absence of resident theatre troupes.[3] Besides the Performing Arts Department which produced the convocation play for the University every November and launched a fiesta of major productions towards the close of every session[4], Olu Obafemi with Ajon Players, Akanji Nasiru with Innovation Theatre, Taiwo Oloruntoba-Oju with African Play-house and Ayo Akinwale used to mount performances on a fairly regular basis. In addition to these were initiatives by student groups. And such efforts, themselves, were not, in any way, infrequent.

But with the exception of the Performing Arts Department and perhaps Ayo Akinwale, all the other groups laid no claim to professionalism. Rather, they were, in the main, experimental, and they enjoyed no subsidies either from the University or from anywhere else. But they managed to keep going nonetheless. However

---

1 An earlier version of this chapter was first published in *Alore: Ilorin Journal of Humanities*. (Vol. 10, No. 1, 1999): 136 – 153

2 These included the Universities of Lagos and Benin as well as Obafemi Awolowo University, Ile Ife.

3 Michael Etherton made this same observation for the Nigerian society in general in the introduction to his book *The Development of African Drama*. (London: Hutchinson & Co., 1982)

4 The play produced during such fiesta comprised of the major projects of the Department's final year students.

one factor united all the producers. And this was their unequivocal belief in the functionalism of theatre, in their position that the substance of any production must have direct relevance for the society. While, however, this is true, it was also the case that the notion of relevance was conceived differently from one producer to another. My aim in this chapter then is to analyze Akanji Nasiru's *Let's Find an Answer*[5] within its context of production, using this as a launching pad for a discussion of the dramatist's production style, his conception of the role of theatre in society and also, what has been perceived through this production as the challenges of amateur production in Nigeria.

Nasiru disbanded the cast which he originally assembled for the production of *Let's Find an Answer* following the indefinite postponement of the workshop for which it was commissioned in 1991. By October of the same year when eventually it held, some members of the original cast had left Ilorin. This was where the playwright-director's problems began – in finding replacements, that is, for some of the key roles. But this is not to suggest that the shift in production date was entirely disadvantageous for the producer. The delay, indeed, allowed Nasiru the opportunity to improve on the manuscript and the versions that emerged afterwards became better defined in terms of focus and more polished in terms of craft. This will be discussed in relative details later.

Doing a play on an area as technical as women reproduction certainly demands painstaking research and Nasiru actually found that he had to peruse a lot of specialized documents and conference reports around the subject he was to produce the play on. This opportunity, as he himself confessed, exposed him to the frightening statistics on maternal deaths and made him appreciate the multidimensional nature of the problem constituting the focus of the international workshop for which the play had been commissioned. For example, one of the teaching hospitals located within the area constituting the focus of the workshop recorded six hundred and twenty four deaths over a period of twelve years. Broken down, it means an average of fitly-two deaths per year or one death a week. Most of the deaths occurred in the rural areas which lacked hospitals, clinics, maternity centres or any kind of modern health facilities. Emergency cases usually became worsened before patients got to the nearest hospital and doctors most often found themselves fighting hopeless battles.

But the question may be asked: why do people often allow such cases to get complicated before heading for the hospital? The answer, simply, is that they are poor and illiterate and ignorant. They are bogged down by superstition. Men marry

5 *Let's Find an Answer* was commissioned for the Sixth Operations Research Workshop on Maternal Mortality originally scheduled to hold in February 1991. The conference had to be postponed due to the crisis that broke open in the Gulf region during the period. When the workshop eventually held in October of the same year, the present writer served as the Assistant Director.

many wives and raise children in numbers and remain tied to traditional methods of child delivery and child care.

Akanji Nasiru knew that the organizers of the conference were not interested in merely publicizing the problem by rehashing the statistics. A lot of discussions had been held on the issue in the past, plenty of paper-work had been done while several letters of appeal for aids and sponsorship had been written to wealthy individuals, philanthropic organizations and relevant governmental and non – governmental agencies. The playwright's challenges then were to offer a viable suggestion and educate people further on the urgency of the problem.

In doing this, Nasiru relies on two major characters in the play that he eventually creates. The first one is Professor who, serving as the playwright's spokesman, proposes the establishment of an experimental rural maternity centre in Korede village; and Funmi Adeola, a young, dynamic lady doctor who is saddled with the responsibility of running the clinic. The series of crises which she regularly battles with attains a climax when the headquarters, finding the solution of instalmental settlement of medical bills which she worked out with the villagers completely unconventional simply halts supply of drugs to her clinic. Illusion merges with reality as another nurse becomes tired of living in a village that is lacking in all basic necessities of life. "What we have been talking about", Funmi Adeola declares in the end, "is not fiction: it is real, and it is still going on." And the problem, Nasiru reiterates, cannot be solved all alone by medical people. Adeola addresses the audience:

Ladies and gentlemen, we cannot pretend any longer...
Even as you are sitting down and watching this, thousands of pregnant women in this country are risking preventable deaths. And there can be no better time than now to speak to everyone who is capable of doing something to help the situation. [6]

A group of villagers soon join Dr Adeola and the issues of agitation become wider and wider. It is only proper, I believe, to let the characters ask their own questions:

1st MAN: Common people are not too backward to know what is good for them. But who takes the pains to provide such good things?
2nd MAN: Government builds mighty houses in towns and big cities, but who thinks of building for us maternity and health centres?
3rd MAN: And roads to link us with civilization.
1st WOMAN: And drugs that our bodies need but our pockets cannot afford?
NURSE: How are we expected to serve happily and
UDOH: consciensciously when we have to do so in environments that endanger our own lives?
NURSE AKIN: How many hundreds of patients can one nurse attend to at a time?

---

6 Akanji Nasiru,*Let's Find an Answer*, 42–43

DOC ADEOLA: The big ones who donate to worthy causes; do they not think that human life is worth giving their wealth to preserve? How many deaths will it take till we know that too many women have died?[7]

This last one, Professor says, is the big question. And the answer, Nasiru says, lies in our hands, in our hearts, and in our will.

The play, it must be said, is comprehensive in the treatment of its subject matter. Nasiru, indeed, has been able to articulate a lot of details in a ninety-minute drama. Details of statistics, of major decisions taken at conferences, major points from research papers, occurrence patterns of maternal deaths, causes, prevention and cure of the mishaps are all transformed into the fictive framework of the dramatic text.

It is pertinent, at this point, to compare the different versions of the script. The first draft bears all the problems of a tentative work. The playwright must have thought that all the information collected from the series of documents he had read must get into the play. The result, thus, is a draft weighed down by crude facts, duly acknowledged quotations, and long lessons on maternal mortality. Two instances should suffice. The first speech is by Professor as he opens the play while the second is by Dr. Adeola while in a meeting with the villagers:

A "We are not here just to publicise a problem. We are here to attack it, to save lives, and to build better ones... We can make this conference the beginning of a new commitment to common decency and common sense". Those words, spoken some two years earlier at the *Nairobi International Conference on Safe Motherhood* began to assume greater significance for me... (my emphasis).[8]

B ...When I examined that young woman, it was clear that she herself had hardly become twenty years old when she became pregnant. How old a woman is before she marries could be a matter of the choice of the people concerned, or there may be a general pattern that is determined by people's practice or belief. But one thing is certain: there is an age when a woman is not yet ripe enough in body and mind to bear the responsibilities of pregnancy and motherhood.[9]

The two speeches are much longer in their original context. But there is no point reproducing them in their entirety. Suffice it to say that many such speeches, especially of the second variety abound in the text. So we are given lectures on what kind of work pregnant women should not do especially when they have reached their sixth or seventh month and why it is not good for them to walk long distances. However by the time Nasiru started re-drafting the work for the October performance, he had become quite confident. He has tamed his fear of plagiarism

7 *Let's Find an Answer*, 43–44
8 Akanji Nasiru, "Let's Find an Answer." First Draft, 3
9 First Draft, 30–31

so that quotations from research papers are now freely integrated into the text of the play. He also brings out his artistic knife and the second speech above is, indeed, one of the casualties. Professor's opening lines are, in addition, broken into four as the playwright invites three consultants to join the elderly man on the Management Board of the Teaching Hospital. Witness Professor directing the words in the first speech quoted above at the members:

> Gentlemen, we are not here just to publicize a problem. We are here to attack it, to save lives, and to build better ones... We can make this meeting the beginning of a new commitment to common decency and common sense. [10]

When Nasiru drops his surgical knife, he picks up the brush and the polish. The lines immediately lose their crudity. They become less direct and more subtle. We notice too that a song has been introduced. "Blowing in the Wind", is a tune for which Nasiru has clear fascination. It is employed in *Come, Let us Reason Together*, an earlier play by him representing his contribution to the search for solution to students crises in the country. In *Let's Find an Answer*, the song is adapted to open and close the performance.

The second version, in turn, became the working script for the cast that eventually produced the play. One of the first things to be noted by the members was that the script – the same village scene particularly – still contained too many long speeches which held the danger of making the performance drag. The director responded by cutting down further on Kabiyesi's and Dr Adeola's speeches in addition to which he worked hard at building a vigorous group response.

Another point of controversy was in the role of Iyalode which survived through to the second version without making any significant contribution. Here, the disagreement was both artistic and ideological. Some people argued that since the problem being discussed related directly to women; Iyalode should have been made a voice for her sex. Others felt that it would create room for variety if some of Baale's speeches were reworked for her. In the end, it was agreed that there was no point for Iyalode's presence if she would have nothing to say. The director eventually edited out the role.

After a number of other minor alterations, Nasiru designed a third draft, the version that went on stage as the premiere production. Professor is the motivator of action. He comes across as a practical, realistic person, a man of ideas. Fellow members of the board understand him. So when he announces that "we are not here to publicize a problem... (But) to attack it... " they know he must have some plans up his sleeves and they are eager to hear him out.

[10] Let's Find an Answer, 3

The man does his homework very well. He understands all the options and possibilities and foresees the questions that may be raised and is thus prepared for them. Nasiru's master stroke is in making him double as narrator. Since they see him as an expert and his efforts at curbing maternal deaths are well appreciated, the spectators are willing to listen to him and he comes out to address them directly. The audience understands his problem, his frustration and his concern. Clearly, Professor inspires Funmi Adeola who herself combines charm and charisma with tact and diplomacy; the qualities with which she wins the loyalty of her team and the confidence of the villagers. The Baale commands the respect of the people because of his mature, straightforward style. Balanced against him are Adio, blunt, harsh and rash; Amusa level-headed but infinitely more devastating and Baba-Soja, the army returnee who inevitably is more enlightened and consequently more shrewd.

The whole play itself is supposed to be a flashback, relayed after the unfortunate death of Baale's daughter. As Professor tells us, the experimental project had been undertaken before the tragic incident occurred and it was supposed to be a major step in the struggle to combat maternal mortality. The intention in the play it backs is to make the audience appreciate the efforts the medical people have made so that others who are equally crucial to the success of the experiment can come in. But Nasiru reverses the situation in the course of the dramatic unfolding, making it now appear as if Baale's daughter's death inspires the establishment of the experimental maternity centre at Korede. This reversal is one of the greatest strengths of the script. It has been so unobtrusively carried out that not a single member of the audience who watched the production in the Banquet Hall A, of Kwara Hotel, Wednesday October 30th, 1991 noticed it. Not many of the people who have since read the script have done so either. [11]

But this is not to suggest that the script is now perfect. In fact the blemishes are yet considerable. Some readers may still find that there is not enough conflict and tension in the script; that the play still depends mainly on long rhetorical speeches. Well, the only word that can be offered in response here is that long speeches delivered like homilies seem to be a characteristic problem of all of Akanji Nasiru's plays to date.

And he himself is probably aware of this. In *Our Survival*, his award-winning play, Nasiru writes as an answer to the question he himself asks on what "the rest of a thirty-man cast (would be doing) while a few characters make elaborate speeches".

---

[11] This assertion is based on the outcome of an informal interview conducted by this writer with some of the members of the audience who watched the production in Kwara Hotel on October 30, 1991 and members of the cast of the production who could be said to have had a close reading of the text.

Group response is vital to the action of the play, and I have indicated in a number of places precisely what other characters should do or say in response to the exhortations, rhetorical questions and rousing speeches of particular characters [12]

It is clear then that Nasiru often relies on group action to compensate for lack of sufficient tension in his plays. It must be acknowledged however that this approach has worked very well in some instances. We recall here the success of the premiere production of *Come, let us Reason Together* in February 1987 where a group of actors and actresses provide mime action to some of the speeches and narrations of the major characters. But the same method did not quite work well for *The Bold Choice*, the play which directly precedes *Come, let us Reason Together*. The first production of the play in late 1985 dragged in spite of the group action. We notice also that Nasiru adopts an easy-way-out approach in some instances where he could have confronted a problem squarely. In starting off, for example, the maternity centre at Korede village, Professor tells us that a "fairly modern building in the village was acquired on a rental basis to serve as maternity space and living quarters for the staff." [13] The reality is that such remote villages often lack such modern structures. Thus, as is my personal view, it would have been more challenging if Nasiru had made Professor and his team to grapple with the problem of space.

It should be noted in addition, that Korede village lacks traditional healers and herbalists and prophets and evangelists who will lay claim to supernatural powers and in whom such simple villagers would have reposed strong faith. It would have been interesting to see Adeola and her team fighting a war of supremacy with these people. Even the traditional birth attendants only get a mention. We do not get to see the kind of resistance they put up against the strange people from the city who have come to deny them of their source of livelihood.

## PRODUCTION EXEGESIS

I have already touched on some of the areas of production in the discussion of the script above. Let us now focus on other aspects of the performance.

The play was produced by Innovation Theatre, a group founded and directed by Akanji Nasiru himself. The theatre is more or less a repertory troupe as most of its productions to date have been scripted by the director himself: *Come, let us Reason Together, Citizen Andrew's Dilemma* and *Love and Strife*, Nasiru's translation into English of Adebayo Faleti's Yoruba play, *Bashorun Gaa*. More important for this discussion however, is the fact that the theatre has no standing troupe.

[12] Akanji Nasiru, *Our Survival*. (London: Macmillan, 1985): iv

[13] *Let's Find an Answer*, 6

This begins to explain why Nasiru found it difficult to replace some of the original members of cast who had to drop out due to one reason or the other.

The method seems to be deliberate though on the part of the director. After all, as a lecturer in Performing Arts, Nasiru could easily have raised a group comprising mainly of his students. Another possible option would have been to, on the other hand, go all out to organize a professional troupe. Not an easy option, as he himself admits, but certainly not totally impossible for him. After all, he has once directed Unilorin Theatre, a troupe which more or less represents the University's first theatre group. Unilorin theatre produced the English version of Kola Ogunmola's *The Palmwine Drinkard* as the University's Convocation play in 1981, and Nasiru's own English translation of Adebayo Faleti's *Basorun Gaa* in 1982. Indeed, Unilorin Theatre owned most of the equipment first inherited by the Performing Arts Department when the latter was established in 1981.

Rather than taking any of the two alternatives above then, Nasiru prefers to raise a fresh cast for every fresh production. First, this has the advantages of demystifying the theatre. Drama arguably precludes nobody. Everybody can, and is free to, participate. And in keeping to this view, the director opens the door of his productions to all enthusiastic people. All an individual requires to participate in a play by Innovation Theatre is a sense of commitment, a readiness to attend rehearsals and a willingness to learn. The result, often, is a mixed cast of academic and non-academic staff both of the University and other tertiary institutions within Ilorin, students from disciplines as wide-ranging as Medicine, Engineering, Education, Social Sciences, and the Arts, and civil servants as well as other categories of workers within Ilorin metropolis. Another reason for preferring this option lies in the troupe's motto: "Art for the Improvement of society." Nasiru explains that if this must be achieved, the people must be made to contribute directly to, and participate actively in, theatre production. Of course, in such an experimental theatre, one should hardly expect an artistically finished and a technically polished production. At the same time however, this should still not suggest sub-standard performances.

The aim is fine but the upsets are often too many. Because for somebody whose only stake in a production lies in his/her enthusiasm, other pressing issues may compel a re-ordering of programme at any point in time. In producing *Let's Find an Answer* then, the director had to re-cast some of the major roles more than twice. At a point, he himself contemplated taking up the part of Funmi Adeola which implies re-interpreting it as a male role. But a young woman eventually came around. Oby Nnanne, at the time a second year student in Education was totally a new comer in the theatre. In choosing her, the director type-cast, his reason being that she carries in her person the energy, dynamism and inspiring confidence required of the lady-obstetrician in the play. Mrs. Nnanne caused the greatest anxiety of the production, expressing loudly her doubt in her ability to learn the lines, and also to carry the role. And this she continued to do even on the last minute of the final rehearsal. The young woman however underwent a sudden transformation on the night of the production as she played her part fairly well.

Such risks could be multiplied over several other members of the cast. But the director, naturally, had always continued, unbending in his determination that things must work out well in the end. And so they have always done. Such risks are not meant for weak stomachs, but the great satisfaction lies in discovering at the end of the experience that a new set of confident people have been delivered for the theatre.

Nasiru's experience demonstrates the hazards of amateur productions in Nigeria and has parallels in other experimental groups. Take Olu Obafemi, founder and director of Ajon Players, a group with a radical bent which used to be based in the Department of Modern European Languages of the same University as another example. Obafemi's departure from Nasiru is that the former tries to retain and maintain a regular cast. The result, in reality, is often only a little better. Quite often, Obafemi has discovered that those whom he regards as most committed and most reliable have let him down at moments most unexpected. With such regular setbacks, only the tough can keep on. And this explains why the Nigerian landscape is arid today when talking in terms of amateur theatre groups.

One other major member of cast must be mentioned. This is Ikem Emordi, the Electronics technician who used to work with the Media Resource Centre at the University of Ibadan – now deceased – who played the role of Professor, a most crucial role in the play as we have seen. In February 1991, when the play was supposed to have been produced, Nasiru had just about two weeks to write and produce the play. To achieve this, the director felt he needed experienced and talented actors. But, according to him, there were not enough hands on ground at Ilorin and so he had to travel to Ibadan to invite Emordi. The man, we must point out, is a versatile man of the theatre having featured in several major productions in Ibadan especially in the 1970's. In addition to his credentials, he also demonstrated great enthusiasm, high sense of commitment and determination towards this particular production. But in practical terms, all these were not often sufficient to bring him often enough from Ibadan to meet rehearsal schedules. The risks involved were many and the anxiety too was great. In the end, the man made the production although, in my view, it was not the best of his performances.

Now to the aspect of staging. What Kwara Hotel offered as the stage is certainly not for play-production as it has neither a backstage nor wings. To compound the problem, the stage is twelve feet deep and disproportionately to a width of forty feet. Yet this was what must be used for the production. What had to be done was to screen off three of the twelve feet depth with flats in order to have something to serve as backstage. Another three feet was also screened off from the width stage-right. There is a window to this side and members who were caught backstage but who had to come in through the auditorium for their next appearance used the window as their exit. Several aspects of the stage instructions on the script also had to be altered. For example, the specified demarcation between the waiting room, consulting room and card room had to collapse and only a simple table and two chairs mark out the doctor's office from the other areas of the maternity centre. There is also a scene where the Korede Women's Cooperative mime working in the fields together with the doctor and the nurses. The mime complements Professor's narration and the script instructs that there should be a spot on him. But since the stage was so small and the apron very close to the audience, Professor had no place where he could stand. His voice had to come over the loudspeakers.

Generally, the production was well-received. It re-opened for the participants at the conference the major issues on maternal mortality. They nodded and chuckled as familiar arguments were re-opened and familiar issues re-played. They grunted to acknowledge their own frustrations and were amused by what they considered as idealistic. They could not help laughing when Funmi Adeola declared that should it happen that the villagers could not settle the cost of the drugs given to them, the money would have to be written off as bad debts.

## AKANJI NASIRU ON THEATRE

Finally, it is necessary to discuss Nasiru's distinctive notion of theatre while evaluating *Let's Find an Answer*. To be sure, the playwright has never missed any opportunity in stating his disagreement with those whom he often describes as "our ideologues who have ready formulas to explain away our social problems,"[14] and who believe that "theatre on its own is capable of bringing about the desired change in society."[15]

Nasiru's reference is clear but my suspicion is that the dramatist may not fully understand the position of the people he is trying to get at. Practitioners of radical theatre in Nigeria do not, as it seems to me, regard the medium in itself as a magic wand kind of solution. Rather, their conviction, and to quote one of them, is predicated on the assumption that "social change could come by the playwright's *ability to raise mass awareness to a positive revolutionary alternative to social*

[14] Akanji Nasiru, *Come let's Reason Together*. (Ijebu Ode: Shebiotimo Publications, 1987): 6

[15] Akanji Nasiru, "The Nigerian Theatre and Community Development: Myth, Reality or Wishful Thinking?" in *The Practice of Community Theatre in Nigeria* ed. Harry Hagher (Lagos: Lobi Consortium, 1991): 52

*decadence"* [16] (my emphasis). If this still remains an offense in any case, it would seem Nasiru himself should be guilty of it. This is because his play *Our Survival* expressly prescribes collective action as the sole alternative to social decadence. I quote Apeena's words of exhortation at the end of the play:

> Let us give our land another chance to become the glorious place that the gods promise us it can be. But let us remember: what we make of it lies in us and us alone. It is in our collective will to progress, to work together, and to resist all forms of oppression and exploitation that our land can be great [17]

It probably needs to be added immediately that Nasiru is not always consistent in this regard. In saying this, the play I have in mind is *The Bold Choice*, his second major work. The script possesses similar potentials for generating mass consciousness as *Our Survival*. But as it runs to a close, the play only invites the military to resolve the crisis generated through a coup. As we move to *Come, let us Reason Together*, the contradiction becomes even stronger. Here, Nasiru stands in the middle, inviting students, vice-chancellors, police and government to come together and find a solution to incessant crises in our higher institutions. He would not take sides, he says, and neither would he dig into the causes. He dismisses as bigoted, the opinion that interprets the conflict as one "between the forces of repression and resistance." [18] Elsewhere, I have pointed out in detail the reactionary tendencies of, and the inherent contradictions, in this particular play [19]. Suffice it to just state it here that the crises, as I understand it, will continue until the establishment learns to come close to the students in order to understand their problems and frustrations.

In this regard then, *Let's Find an Answer* has certain things in common with *Come, let us Reason* and demonstrates even more profoundly what seems to me to represent the contradictory tendencies in Nasiru's perspectives. At the end of the play, the people come out in agitation, not against government but against the "big ones who donate to worthy causes" asking: "Why can we not with equal zeal build maternity and health centres to save human souls here on earth?" [20]

Nasiru describes as simplistic, even puerile, any opinion that heaps the responsibility for the situation on government. I think he misses the point. Because, as I believe, a government has no purpose if it cannot provide its citizens with

---

16 Olu Obafemi, "Revolutionary Aesthetics in Recent Nigerian Theatre." In *African Literature Today*, (Vol. 12, 1982): 119

17 *Our Survival*, 38

18 *Come, Let us Reason*, 6

19 Wumi Raji, "Triumph of Form in Come, Let us Reason." In *The Herald*. (February 24, 1987): 12

20 *Let's Find an Answer*, 44

such basic essentials as water, roads, light, education and health. Most rural communities from where we get our food and raw materials lack most of these basic things. Let us ask Nasiru how many of the problems our wealthy individuals and philanthropic organizations can, and will be ready to, solve and in how many of the villages? The playwright is grateful to the "kind people outside our land who are not happy that our mothers suffer so much in the process of bringing children into the world"[21] and have therefore provided us with aids. This, to use Ngugi's words, is standing reality on its head:

> Africa's natural and human resources continue to develop Europe and America: but Africa is made to feel grateful for aid from the same quarters that still sit on the back of the continent.[22]

Let's wind up by submitting that to the extent that the people are made to be dependent upon the goodwill and support of other groups, to that extent will they remain vulnerable to their domination and manipulation. Alternatively then, the suggestion should be to encourage them to struggle towards a different kind of society where the problem will be those of everybody and the search for solution will involve all. In doing this though, the fact must be borne in mind that there is no human system without its own problems and contradictions!

---

[21] *Let's Find an Answer*, 28

[22] Ngugi wa Thiong'o, *Decolonising the Mind: The Politics of Language in African Literature.* (London: James Currey, 1986): 29

## WORKS CITED

Etherton, Michael. *The Development of African Drama* (London: Hutchinson & Co., 1982).

Obafemi, Olu. "Revolutionary Aesthetics in Recent Nigerian Theatre." *African Literature Today*. (Vol. 12, 1982): 144 – 115.

Olorunyomi, Dapo. "Come, Let us Reason Together: A Review" *The Herald* (Saturday February 28, 1987): 12.

Nasiru, Akanji. *Come, Let us Reason Together* (Ijebu Ode: Shebiotimo Publications, 1987).

– "Let's Find an Answer" (Unpublished Manuscript).

– "The Nigerian Theatre and Community Development: Myth, Reality or Wishful Thinking?" in *The Practice of Community Theatre in Nigeria* ed. Harry Hagher (Lagos: Lobi Consortium, 1991): 47 – 54.

– *Our Survival* (London: Machmillan, 1985).

Ngugi Wa Thiong'o. *Decolonising the Mind: The Politics of Language in African Literature* (London: James Currey, 1986).

Raji, Wumi. "The Triumph of Form in *Come, let us Reason*" *The Herald*. (February 24, 1987): 12.

# Chapter 6

# Style and Postcolonial Respresentation in the Plays of Niyi Osundare[1]

> We must smash this wall
> Built of the inequities
> Of class and crime
> Then shake new hands
> Over the ashes of severance[2]

It appears I was able to touch that man, and his coming also touched me.[3]

When he first announced his plans to publish an edited volume of essays on the works of Niyi Osundare in 1999, it was almost certain that AbdulRasheed Na'Allah never contemplated including a chapter on Osundare's plays in what would later become *The People's Poet: Emerging Perspectives on Niyi Osundare*.[4] Though clearly aware that the subject of the book once tried his hands at writing drama, the editor made it clear both through his choice of a tentative title and the advertisement that went to prospective contributors that he intended the volume to be devoted solely to Osundare's poetry.[5] So "total" is his acceptance as a poet that many people do not consider it worthwhile to explore other aspects of Osundare's intellectual and literary efforts.

---

1 An earlier version of this paper was published in AbdulRasheed Na'Allah ed., *The People's Poet: Emerging Perspectives on Niyi Osundare*. (Trenton, NJ: Africa World Press, 2002): 527 – 535

2 Excerpted from Niyi Osundare's "A Reunion," one of the poems in *Village Voices,* Osundare's second collection of poetry. See Niyi Osundare, *Village Voices*. (Ibadan: Evans, 1984): 14

3 This was Niyi Osundare in an interview with Stephen Arnold. See Stephen Arnold, "A People's Persona: Autobiography, Post – Modernism and the Poetry of Niyi Osundare," in *Autobiographical Genres in Africa* ed. Ulla Schild (Mainz – Afrika Studien, 1996): 34

4 See AbdulRasheed Na'Allah ed. *The People's Poet: Emerging Perspectives on Niyi Osundare*. (Trenton, NJ: Africa World Press, 2002)

5 The first paragraph of the call for contributions to the book reads in part: "This is introducing a book project on the poetry and life of Niyi Osundare, award – winning Nigerian poet, essayist, playwright and human rights crusader. The book tentatively titled 'The Total Poet,' intends to explore Osundare's poetics..." See AbdulRasheed Na;Allah' "Call for Papers."

Or this probably is not the case with regards to the drama. Many people simply do not know that Osundare has ever written a play. This much was admitted by many of the spectators of *The State Visit*, Osundare's play mounted during his fiftieth birthday celebration held at the University of Ibadan, Nigeria between 11th and 13th March, 1997. They had certainly never paid complete attention – if ever they paid any at all – to the blurbs of *Songs of the Market Place* and *Village Voices* both of which at least acknowledged that the celebrated poet had some unpublished plays, one of which was performed to mark twenty years of television in Africa in 1979!

There is a tinge of irony to this situation. Because, as he revealed in a hint he dropped during a private discussion with this writer, Osundare would most probably have preferred to be a playwright but for the intimidating talents of Femi Osofisan, his close friend and ideological soul mate. Though he started writing poetry since as early as his days in secondary school, what Stephen Arnold has so accurately described as Osundare's 'civic consciousness' [6] would have made him prefer the more public and more communal opportunities offered by the medium of theatre. This could be why, indeed, as soon as he returned from Toronto in 1979, he settled down to play writing, completing work on two manuscripts that single year, and producing one of them even as he commenced work on the third. By this time, Osofisan had already established himself as the foremost Nigerian dramatist of the generation after Soyinka, having produced such important plays as *The Chattering and the Song, Once Upon Four Robbers, Who is Afraid of Solarin* and *Morountodun*, among others. Osundare himself acknowledge his friend's achievements in a review of one of the plays in *West Africa* in 1980. [7] Probably because of this, the Ikere-born stylistician simply packed up his play scripts after completing work on *The State Visit* in 1981, returning fully to poetry, a field where he won his first prize in 1968. This chapter exhumes the three plays that Osundare drafted before taking a decision to face poetry in full – *The Wedding Car, The Man Who Walked Away* and *The State Visit* – exploring their thematic engagements and their technical potentials as well as limitations, and locating them, in general, within the context of Osundare's oeuvre.

"A Reunion", the poem from which the first epigraph to this chapter has been excerpted is an autobiographical poem which this writer has described else where as articulating the theme of Osundare's career. [8] The poem presents two charac-

6 See Stephen Arnold, "A People Persona," 35

7 In "Social Message of a Nigerian Playwright," Niyi Osundare declares that Femi Osofisan is "already doing for us (Africans) what Bertolt Brecht did for Europe." See *West Africa*. (Jan. 28, 1980): 147 – 150

8 See Wumi Raji, "A Feast of Reunion" Citation Read in Honour of Niyi Osundare at his Fiftieth Birthday Anniversary, 12 March, 1997." *ALA Bulletin: A Publication of the African Literature*

ters: the persona who, having traversed the Atlantic in search of the golden fleece now finds himself as a member of the class of the bourgeoisie; and the addressee whose dream has been betrayed as a consequence of poverty, and who now is as "scorched as a sponge." The epigraph, which represents the closing lines of the poem, expresses the desire of the new arrival to smash the wall now separating him from his friend and re-establish the relationship that originally existed between the two of them. 'A Reunion" is an old poem capturing an actual encounter of 1974, an encounter so moving as to bolster Osundare's ideological convictions, the formative stage of which could be traced to the poet's communal origins. [9] "A Reunion" is the poem that led to that "unbreakable pledge" by Osundare [10] to remain committed to the deprived of the earth. It is the point of this chapter that stylistically and thematically, Osundare's three play scripts represent unequivocal affirmation of this pledge.

A society wedding stands as the core action in *The Wedding Car*. To be sure, a typical wedding programme in contemporary Nigerian society itself represents a veritable study in postcolonial culture. The wedding price, the attire donned by the participants, the manner of entertainment presented, as well as the actual rituals of wedding, are all fusions of traditional heritage and "modern" practices. But perhaps more important for the playwright here is the characteristic ostentatiousness and superficiality often associated with the programme. And Osundare's position is very clear on this. "Must I starve because my brother's son is getting married?", so retorts a member of the bridegroom's entourage when asked to make a contribution at the engagement ceremony. The man is one with Osundare in expressing outrage and indignation against the people who "live in an ocean of wealth" even as majority of the people wallow in abject poverty. Chief Chamberlains, as the complete embodiment of this artificiality and vanity, is the consistent target of derision and wit. His ultimate disgrace is not just as a consequence of smuggling a car into the country but also because of the innumerable crimes which he has perpetrated against the dispossessed of the earth.

But it is very important to pass a comment on the role of Lasun in the play. Given the general atmosphere of despair, of dashed hopes and frustration, it is

---

*Association*. 24.2 Spring 1998

9 In a 1990 interview with Stephen Arnold, Osundare, in answering a question on why he is a socialist, has declared thus: "I think I had practiced the socialism that I grew up to read about even before I was literate at all. I grew up in a communal situation. I never saw anybody starve. I never saw anybody have too much while the other person had nothing." See Stephen Arnold, "A People's Persona." 37

10 In place of a prefatory note to the first edition of *Songs of the Market Place*, Osundare's first collection of poetry, is the following quotation from Pablo Neruda: "I made an unbreakable pledge to myself: that the people would find their voices in my song." See Niyi Osundare, *Songs of the Market Place*. Ibadan: New Horn, 1983): vii

understandable that certain ideologically committed intellectuals would begin to experience a slide. Deremi epitomizes this in the play. His desperation to break the cycle of poverty explains why he has to cross over to seek a wife from the Chamberlains. Osundare insists however that to so compromise is to lose one's cherished freedom; it is to embark on a course of self-destruction. Lasun is that character in the play who takes Deremi on a journey down the memory lane. "What happened to the dream we had," he asked Deremi at long last:

> the dreams we nursed together as students at the University? I could remember we looked all around our society and what we saw were the monsters of greed and graft, of inefficiency, of lack of consideration for others, of the deification of money and property. We decided to be different. It was a solemn pledge to let the world know there is a healthy alternative; that ours was not a society irredeemably bound to ruin. What happened? Are those bow ties and tailcoats part of these dreams? Is this desperate bid to be son-in-law to a filthy millionaire part of that dream? [11]

So many questions. But are the answers so easy? Would Lasun also be able to claim just like Osundare does in the second epigraph that he "was able to touch that man?"

Beyond this level of rhetorics however, there is a definite point through which the second epigraph ties up with both "The Wedding Car" and "The Man Who Walked Away," Osundare's second play script. As one of the examples used to illustrate his argument on the relevance of Osundare's life to his poetry, Stephen Arnold has, in "A Peopled Persona: Autobiography, Post-Modernism and the Poetry of Niyi Osundare" the same essay that I have continued to refer to, cited another excerpt from a 1990 interview he had with the poet. In the excerpt, Osundare talks of how a man, having been fired from the job he has held for twenty years following the introduction in the mid eighties of the Structural Adjustment Programme (SAP) in Nigeria, decided to commit suicide. Somehow, however, the man stumbles on Osundare's newspaper poem titled "Retrenched" and, having read it, decided to change his mind. The man thought that "he shouldn't die and allow the enemy to triumph." [12] The relationship between this incident and "The Wedding Car" is figurative. For somebody like Deremi to marry Chief Chamberlains' daughter will be to commit ideological suicide and is an event over which the enemies will rejoice. This is why Lasun warns him (Deremi) to "take care not to stumble", and why Tunji the best man accepts that though the pressure may be overwhelming, "victory lies in not yielding." [13]

---

11 Niyi Osundare, "The Wedding Car." Unpublished manuscript, 34

12 Stephen Arnold, "A People's Persona," 156

13 "The Wedding Car," 36

On its own, "The Man Who Walked Away" stands as a fictive anticipation of the event of the late eighties with the simple difference being that Deji, the central character in the play, does not have the benefit of the insight that "Retrenched" has to offer. Read in another way, the poem which has now been included in *Songs of the Season*, the published selection from the "experimental weekly poetry column" in The Nigerian Tribune can be described as a re-written version of the play script of 1979.

To be sure, the odds against Deji, are extremely enormous. The multi-national company with which he works launches the first assault by laying him off. The landlord follows suit by harassing him for not being able to pay his rents. Iya Agba the mother-in-law jeers at him for his inability to provide the basic needs of his family. At the night club, Chief Kogbade Jones, government contractor and imperialist ally, announces boldly that he could not be bothered about the deprived of the earth. And, to cap it all, Deji finds himself treated like a leper in the labour office. Very terrible experience, no doubt, but they seem hardly sufficient for somebody who has hope as his guiding philosophy [14] to resolve to take his own life: somebody who is clear-headed enough to be able to distinguish between what is, and what ought to be, who has an understanding wife and two extremely promising children; is it correct for such a person to die just like that? Osundare must have re-read "The Man Who Walked Away" in the eighties. He must have felt uncomfortable with the hero who simply chickens out and, as a consequence, must have decided to re-design Deji's fate. "Retrenched" ends with a four-line stanza, on a note of determination:

> My wife is wan, my kids are old
> The times are hard, but so my hear
> I will never die on the rubbish heap
> I've sowed my sweat, I deserve to reap. [15]

It is important to make it clear that "The Man Who Walked Away" does not, everything taken together, end on a pessimistic note. As pointed out just a while ago, Deji has two extremely promising children and a highly determined wife. As light fades out slowly at the end of the play, Osundare takes time to make it clear that the three survivors will hold out firmly and strongly. Thus, as Abeke bursts out into profuse weeping following the confirmation of Deji's death on the news, she reaches out to Toyin and Sola, pressing "them close to her breast". The

---

[14] Part of the stage instruction at the beginning of "The Man who Walked Away" reads: "In the centre of the back wall is hung a cardboard chart on which the following is boldly printed: 'Motto – When Their's Life – Their's Hope.'" See Niyi Osundare: "The Man who Walked Away." (unpublished manuscript): 2

[15] Niyi Osundare, *Songs of the Season*. (Ibadan: Heinemann, 1990): 20

male child is not even bothered about the present. His face, as the stage instruction makes it clear "is dry, firm and far." [16]

*The State Visit* is by far the most ambitious of the three play-scripts. It is also the most adventurous. In its adoption of the story-telling technique, Osundare betrays the influence on him of Femi Osofisan, his more accomplished playwright friend. And in its savage criticism of African dictators and the close depiction of their vices and absurdities, the script also reminds us of Wole Soyinka's *Opera Wonyosi* and *A Play of Giants*.

The play, indeed, represents a consummation of the dreams conceived in the first two works, taking the reader, as it were, into the distance that Sola, the younger of Deji's two children in "The Man Who Walked Away" gazes at during the close of the play. Though written, as already stated, since as far back as 1981, the play was first performed at the Arts Theatre, University of Ibadan, between January 10 and 12, 1997 under the direction of Wale Oyinlola. The production was resurrected in March of the same year, becoming part of the programme put together to mark Osundare's fiftieth birthday. In 2002, it was issued by Kraft Books, Ibadan, Nigeria, thus becoming the first ever of Osundare's plays to be published.

*The State Visit* is different from the two earlier works which have their actions played out in domestic environments as the author, this time around, utilizes a public metaphor. The work is set in a fictive country of Yanke, a state that is under the firm grip of a vicious dictator. Right from the point when the play opens, the audience is transformed into the epicentre of power. A fellow predator is being expected from a neighbouring jungle, a reason for which the lion of Yanke has summoned members of his family to a meeting. Osundare's sense of rage and indignation is very clear in the stage instruction.

> The stage is set for a State Cabinet meeting. Downstage centre, somebody who looks like the Head of State is seated on a throne-like chair with a prominent back rest and gold-plated arm rests. The Head... is chronically obese, and slumps in his monumental chair, breathing hard. He is in an army uniform, preferably fatigue but his hat is placed on the table before him, while the belt disappears in the generous folds of flesh making up his abdomen. [17]

The cabinet members themselves are a fawning, sycophantic lot. With the exception of the Minister of Finance, all of the others simply consent to whatever proposal the Head puts forward. The meeting itself has a one – item agenda and this, directly, is on how to generate the funds needed to welcome the visiting President of Wilama. In the end, the minister of Finance is directed to divert a special fund

16 "The Man who Walked Away," 28

17 Niyi Osundare, *The State Visit*. (Ibadan: Kraft Books, 2002): 9

into the project. Finding this difficult to accede to, he takes a decision to resign his portfolio. And going by the discussion that follows his exit from the meeting, it seems clear as well that he may pay the supreme price for his audacity.

Act II introduces the audience to the other side of Yanke. Here the ordinary run of humanity, the beggars especially, are brought out to narrate their stories. Most harrowing of the stories is that of Abeke, the blind woman who was raped by an unknown individual, an encounter which produces the child she now carries. The play ends with the people launching a protest against the profligacy of the state, against misrule, against dictatorship. The state responds by opening fire on them. In Act V, the narrator returns to the stage to present the audience with his final comments. "What you have just seen is a short chapter in a l-o-n-g dream," says he:

> The people have shown their anger; the guns have answered. The outcome is so dramatically obvious. But Yankeland will never be the same again. In every village, every hamlet, the questions raised here are fledgling into birds which perch on every roof. Questions too many for the steel muzzle of the gun. The days of the lion are numbered. [18]

The three plays explored here belong, as already stated, in the early stage of Osundare's career as a writer. At this time, the man himself was young and his passion, strong- very strong. There is no doubt that his blood boiled with the fire of idealism. And this is to the extent that he sometimes allows it to overwhelm him and bring down his art. Take *The Wedding Car* as an example. The manner of ending that play represents a typical instance of deux ex machina. Chief Chamberlains', up till the last scene, has certainly been having his way. He is, as the man himself would have put it, enjoying his hard-earned wealth. Part of this "enjoyment" is the expensive wedding ceremony that he has organized for his daughter. It is at the peak of this ceremony that two customs officials appear to effect the man's arrest – and for an offence as *ordinary* as smuggling a car into the country! The word "ordinary" has been so emphasized because the sociological environment of the play is one which permits such "highly – placed" people to get away with even much weightier offences and crimes. In fact, in the immediately preceding scene, we encounter three erstwhile idealists as they express their frustrations and despair. Tunji's words which end that scene talks of the difficulties of living in "a world of reactionary conformism which keeps beckoning you to come over to join in, to fall in line." [19] What magical developments have then taken place so suddenly, altering the world so radically? From which planet could the two uniformed men have descended that they could possess the temerity to disrupt such an important occasion?

[18] *The State Visit*, 64

[19] "The Wedding Car", 37

Similar questions could also be posed regarding *The State Visit*. Indeed, given the story-line up till the end of Act III, there is no soothsayer who, if consulted, would have risked predicting the kind of developments that the reader confronts in Act IV. This is because, up to that point, the lion of Yanke is still firmly in the saddle, he is in absolute control. There is no information at all about the collective of workers, artisans, women, students and beggars who take over the stage in the following scene. There is, in fact, no prior hint of any form of organized opposition. It is certainly salutary for the playwright to propose an alternative to the prevailing obsolescence but it seems more important to be able to logically lead the audience along such direction.

It is necessary to establish an inter-section between the point made above and an even more fundamental weakness of Osundare's play scripts; which weakness may not be unconnected with the fact that the Ikere-born author is actually, instinctively, a poet.

Like the novel, modern poetry is largely introverted, privately addressed, as it were, from the writer to the reader. Well, due to the heavy influence on him of his indigenous heritage, Osundare's own verses are presented in such a way that they could be accompanied with traditional musical instruments, in such a way that they could be chanted and performed. In spite of this however, virtually all the works still remain as poetry in the modern sense, they still remain essentially monologic, still lacking in conflicts and movements, the principal ingredients of drama.

The terms, "conflicts" and "movements," have been deliberately employed here especially against the word "dialogue" which is often considered to be the most important element of the dramatic form. No doubt, dialogue is important in a play but it of itself does not constitute the drama. In fact, in the context of theatre, dialogue can become monologic especially if it is not propelled by conflicts and actions. The former element actually lies at the heart of any dramatic enactment and it can be open or hidden, and can be established within the mind of an actor or actress, in-between actors and actresses and in between groups of actors and actresses. What sustains it is the existence of an issue over which the opposing forces in the play contend.

Let me explain. Sontri in Femi Osofisan's *The Chattering and the Song*[20] has a problem with the state, with the prevailing order in it; and is therefore engaged in a struggle to destabilize it. But this is not the issue in the play. The issue, at least at the immediate level of analysis, is Yajin. She is the factor responsible for the rivalry between Mokan and Sontri, and it is in an attempt to even up with the latter on this factor that Mokan enlists in the service of the state. Sontri himself

[20] Femi Osofisan, *The Chattering and the Song*. (Ibadan: Ibadan University Press, 1977)

could become the point of conflict at another level of analysis. Because he constitutes a threat to it, the state wants him arrested. The revolutionary movement together with which he works continues to shield him. The important question then becomes that of whether or not he will be caught and if he will, when, and under what circumstances.

To be sure, Osundare's play scripts possess great potentialities for actions. Clear evidences of this abound in the sharp oppositional relationships which often exist between his characters, in how he places heavy psychological burden on some of them and in the very clear contrasts he often draws between their principles and aspirations. What is always lacking however is an element that will bring the different forces together in a struggle.

It is probably necessary to reiterate the point here that the struggle being talked about does not have to be physical or open, even. The struggle over Sidi, for example, in Wole Soyinka's *The Lion and the Jewel,* [21] is an intense one, a very intense one at that. Yet, and throughout the play, the two antagonists come face – to – face only once. Even this encounter is a brief one, and it does not go beyond, at least on the surface, an exchange of greetings by the two. In my view, Osundare needs to find a way of closing the space that is often created between the different forces that he often delineates in his dramatic works. He ought to have devised something that would, for example, brought Deji and his tormentors out in a confrontation in "The Man who Walked Away." Similarly, instead of having the customs officials do the job for them, Lasun, Deremi and Tunji who, collectively, embody the alternative principle in "The Wedding Car" also need to have a point of engagement with Chief Chamberlains. Once the two parties engage each other over an issue, the play could have ended with the lot falling on either of the two sides, or on a note of impasse. When, however, there is no factor of conflict, the danger for monologism arises in a play, as a single party ends up dominating the dramatic space. This is why Deji, in spite of being the central character in "The Man Who Walked Away" exerts very little presence on stage; and why the trio of Lasun, Deremi and Tunji in "The Wedding Car" are consigned to the most peripheral position in the play.

Perhaps because it is the most ambitious of the three plays, the point being discussed comes out most boldly in *The State Visit*. The play is about political dictatorship and corruption in Africa, as already said. But so, as well, is Wole Soyinka's *Opera Wonyosi.* [22] In the latter play, the primary struggle is between Anikura and Macheath, and it is over Polly, the former's daughter. Because Anikura does not want to have Macheath as his son – in – law, he plots to have him eliminated.

[21] Wole Soyinka, *The Lion and the Jewel* in *Wole Soyinka: Collected Plays II*. (Oxford: Oxford University Press, 1981): 1 – 58

[22] Wole Soyinka, *Opera Wonyosi*. (London: Rex Collins, 1981)

This is the simple story at the centre of the play. All the other issues raised in it are woven around this central conflict. In my view, *The State Visit* does not seem to have such organizing conflict at its core. In Acts I and III, Head and members of his cabinet hold long meetings, working out details of a reception programme for a Head of State who will be visiting from another country. In neither of these two scenes do we get any hint as regards the existence of a resistance group. We encounter, of course, the beggars in Act II and we get to learn of their troubles and plight. It is clear however that they are a totally helpless, powerless lot. Now in Act IV, and without any warning whatsoever, workers, students, women, beggars, etc, invade the stage in protest against the state. A set of questions present themselves here: Where have they emerged from? Who is their leader? What are the immediate issues in contention?

This returns me again to Femi Osofisan. In his *Morountodun*, [23] the initial confrontation between the farmers and the state is set off over taxation. The former, feeling that they get nothing in return for the exorbitant contribution they make to the state, form a united front saying "no, no more." As the struggle heats up, the leader of the farmers' struggle becomes the issue, with the state feeling that once it succeeds in capturing the leader, the struggle will end. This then is where Titubi comes in, and where the story of Moremi becomes relevant. In *The State Visit*, the minister of Finance and the painter, the two people who initially resist the attempt by the state to coerce them do so as separate individuals. Because they are not connected to any forces or movement, the state has no problem getting rid of them. What happens in Act IV then is another instance of deux ex machina – more or less. And this kind of situation is almost totally inevitable once there is no organizing element of struggle in a play.

Be that as it may, Osundare's dramatic works are welcome addition to his poetic output. In spite of the flaws highlighted above, the scripts, taken together, still hold out some promise. Thematically, they integrate with the poetry in exploring the possibilities of hope. Formally, they exploit and refine the resources of traditional heritage, fusing them with modern techniques. All Osundare needs to do is just apply himself a little more to the form, and indeed take pain to investigate and master the nature and function of conflict and action in drama. Once this is done, he will be on the way to establishing a major presence in the genre of performance art.

---

23 Femi Osofisan, *Morountodun*. (Lagos: Longman, 1982)

## WORKS CITED

Arnold, Stephen "A Peopled Persona: Autobiography, Post-Modernism and the Poetry of Niyi Osundare." Autobiographical Genres in Africa. (Mainz – Bayreuth: Africa Studien, 1996).

Osofisan, Femi. *The Chattering and the Song*. (Ibadan: Ibadan University Press, 1977)

– *Morountodun*. (Lagos: Longman, 1982)

Osundare, Niyi. "The Man Who Walked Away." Unpublished Manuscript.

– "Social Message of a Nigerian Playwright" *West Africa*, (Jan 28, 1980): 147–150.

– *Songs of the Market place*. (Ibadan: New Horn, 1983).

– *Songs of the Season*. (Ibadan: Heinemann, 1990).

– "The State Visit." Unpublished Manuscript.

– *Village Voices*. (Ibadan: Evans, 1984).

– "The Wedding Car." Unpublished Manuscript.

Raji, Wumi "A Feast of Reunion: Citation Read in Honour of Niyi Osundare at His Fiftieth Birthday Anniversary, 12 March, 1997." *ALA Bulletin* 24.2 Spring 1998.

Soyinka, Wole. *A Play of Giants*. (Ibadan: Spectrum Books, 1984).

– *The Lion and the Jewel* in *Wole Soyinka: Collected Plays II* (Oxford: Oxford University Press, 1981): 1–58

– *Opera Wonyosi*. (London: Rex Collins, 1981)

# CHAPTER 7

# URBAN DISLOCATION AND POST-COLONIAL TRANSFORMATION IN THE PLAYS OF FEMI OSOFISAN

The modern city fascinates and repels. And all analysts are agreed on this. Be they from the perspectives of geographers, sociologists, architects, town-planners or social workers, reactions to contemporary urban settlements have always been characterized by ambivalence and ambiguities. The city generates hope; it celebrates love and indeed, proffers innumerable wonders. But the same city engenders despair and loneliness, destroys great dreams and promotes chaos and crimes. Write Michael P. Weber and Anne Lloyd as they struggle to capture the image of the contemporary American city:

> City planners talk about an urban crisis that cannot be solved without drastic action. Inner city residents complain of rundown housing, poor schools, lack of jobs, and a variety of other shortcomings. On the other hands young professional people point to the cultural, intellectual and recreational advantages of urban life. The sub-urban business person-commuter however speaks of job opportunities while decrying morning and evening traffic jam, pollution and crime in the streets. Yet all of these people, along with 150 million other Americans continue to live in urban area. [1]

This picture of the American city is applicable, albeit with modifications, to all cities of contemporary capitalist societies. And Alan Gilbert and Josef Gugler would readily support this. In their jointly-authored book, they locate the logic of this universalism in modern technology, the transnational "price mechanism," international finance system and 'real estate institutions.' [2] All of these factors create "a distinctive pattern of land use with population densities and land price gradients, central business districts, high class sub-urban residential areas and inner city slums." [3]

---

1 Michael P. Weber & Anne Lloyd, *The American City*. (St. Paul West Publishing Co, 1975): 3

2 Alan Gilbert & Josef Gugler, *Cities, Poverty and Development: Urbanization in the Third World*. (New York: Oxford University Press, 1975): 24

3 *Cities, Poverty and Development*, 25

But while this is true, it is also the case that a great disparity exists between city conditions of the metropolitan centres of the world on the one hand, and those of peripheral societies on the other. Gilbert and Gugler also make this point with some force. The Third World city, as the authors argue, stands desperately marginalized in a world economy that is structurally monopolistic and unequal. The Western world calls the shot when it comes to crucial policy decision-making on science, technology and economy. And the Third World only acquiesces meekly. The result of this lopsidedness is dislocation, a reality that Gilbert illustrates graphically in his essay 'Urban Development in a World System':

> In the third World City, the relative poverty of the Black Baltimore slumdweller is accentuated by absolute material deprivation. Some poor people in the United States suffer from malnutrition; most of the poor in Indian cities fall into this category. Overcrowded tenement slums and too few jobs are abhorrent, but the lack of fresh water, medical services, drainage and unemployment compensation adds to this problem in most third world cities. Without wishing to paint Dickensian pictures of squalor, poverty and crime, it is far too easy to sketch the outline of a basically unfair and degrading situation. [4]

It seems interesting, how Gilbert ends his point by referring to a writer. Indeed, most creative works, guardedly speaking, represent studies in Geography, Sociology, Urban Economics, Politics and Estate Management put together. The responses consequently projected range from outright rejection of city conditions, to complete acceptance of its forms, or a critical engagement with its order. Thus, while Charles Dickens is filled with revulsion for the London of Victorian era, Carl Sandberg composes poems in endless celebration of the city of Industrial America. [5] The image painted by James Joyce of Dublin in his The Dubliners is so vivid and so graphic that it is almost possible to form a fairly accurate image of the city without ever having visited the place. And this much can also be said of J.P. Clark's 'Ibadan', a poem which, in short lines, captures the tension that inevitably generates when the 'running splash' of old ways intersects with the 'gold' of newness. [6]

If other writers are not as accurate in their depiction of physical contours of different urban agglomerations, it does not necessarily suggest that they are less engaged with citiness and its ambiguities. Besides his series of autobiography,

---

4 Gilbert, Alan, "Urban Development in a World System," in *Cities, Poverty and Development: Urbanization in the Third World*, ed. Alan Gilbert & Josef Gugler (New York: Oxford University Press, 1975): 25

5 The poems collected in Sandberg's *Chicago Poems* are essentially devoted to a celebration of Chicago, the beautiful capital of Illinois. See Carl Sandberg, *Chicago Poems* (New York: Atheneum, 1963).

6 J.P. Clark, "Ibadan," in *Poems of Black Africa*, (ed.) Wole Soyinka (London: Heinemanns, 1975): 142

hardly does Soyinka cite the name of any major city in his works. Yet we do not fail to recognize his engagement with urban contradictions in his works. Take *The Road* for example. The dominating set-prop is a physical symbolization of problematic urbanity. The 'bolekaja' [7] is ill-balanced and completely without wheels. Here we get a clear picture of halted motion. Murano was knocked down by a lorry while in a state of transition. Being mute, he becomes a physical representation of indeterminacy, of disarticulation. The layabouts, trapped as they all are in the "Aksident Store," complete for us the picture of an urban formation that is held in a state of suspension, of dislocation and disorientation.

To Ngugi wa Thiong'o, the chaos and violence of the modern city in Kenya has its roots in a bourgeoisie that prefers to subordinate the interest of the people to that of the transnational corporations, and who feel proud of their status as inheritors of the colonial legacy of land expropriation and capital accumulation. We remember how the Member of Parliament plays out Gikonyo in *A Grain of Wheat* as the latter struggles to purchase a parcel of land in Nairobi, [8] and how Munira, Wanja and Abdulla are in *Petals of Blood* [9] eventually consigned to the periphery of the social formation in modern Illmorog, a city that developed out of their sweat and determination.

The pattern of analysis being pursued here would seem to hold the possibility of leading us to a cul-de sac. This, precisely, is with regards to our chosen authors' disposition towards citiness. Because, while Osofisan's commitment to post-colonial transformation can hardly be doubted, it may be argued that city pictures have not always featured in his works. Indeed, with the exception of *Once Upon Four Robbers* [10], and one or two other plays perhaps, most of Osofisan's published major plays are set in the rural past. So, where Lagos is readily recog-

---

7 'Bolekaja,' a Yoruba word which, literally translated, means 'come down and let us fight' is the name by which the popular passenger bus in Lagos, the commercial capital of Nigeria is known. In *The Road*, Soyinka makes one such grounded bus the dominating set – prop of the play. Part of the play's opening instruction reads: 'thrusting downstage from a corner of the shack is the back of a 'bolekaja' (Mammy Wagon), lop – sided and minus its wheels.' See Wole Soyinka, *Collected Plays* (Oxford: Oxford University Press, 1973): 151

8 Ngugi wa Thiong'o, *A Grain of Wheat* (London: Heinemann, 1967)

9 Munira, Wanja and Abdulla are the three city people who first settled in Illmorog at a time when it was simply a forgotten village. When eventually urbanization catches up with the place, all three but with the exception of Wanja are relegated to the margins of the city formation. See Ngugi wa Thiong'o *Petals of Blood* (London: Heinemanns, 1977)

10 *Once Upon Four Robbers* directly examines the phenomenon of armed robbery in Nigerian cities. Femi Osofisan argues in the play that the 'legalized slaughtering' of armed robbers will not solve the problem of violent robbery. According to him, 'It is obvious that as long as a single daring nocturnal trip with a gun or a matchet can yield the equivalent of one man's annual income, we shall continue to manufacture our own potential assassins.' See Femi Osofisan *Once Upon Four Robbers* (Ibadan: Heinemann Books), 1991

nizable in most locations of Cyprian Ekwensi's works, where Sembene Ousmane will not hesitate to paint a graphic picture of Dakar and La Guma of Johannesburg, and where the city of Port Harcourt is openly announced in Rotimi's *If*, the image that often confronts the reader in any typical setting of most of Osofisan's works is that of the traditional community complete, quite often, with its rites and rituals, its festivals and taboos, and in short, its homogeneity.

One small argument to propose against this may be that in escaping always to the rural setting, the playwright has indicated his rejection of the city and its orders. But, as has been indicated, this will be too small and too cheap. My position in this chapter, therefore, is that in those lines which seem to project the traditional village formation in a typical play by Femi Osofisan, are actually etched the physical pictures of the modern city. Even at the surface level, Osofisan drops hints as regard the images he paints: that they are not of the old ethos but of contemporary urban locations. Readers or audiences miss this however as a result of their absorption in the dramatists' often powerfully crafted actions and stories. I illustrate this argument with two plays of Osofisan of the early eighties. *No More the Wasted Breed* and *Esu and the Vagabond Minstrels.* [11]

*No More the Wasted Breed* is set in a riverine location. The inhabitants of the community are in the throes of a plague. The waters of the rivers have crashed over the banks and have invaded the farmlands, and the houses. Strange times, so the people say, especially with food supply that is in acute shortage, with crops that have all rotted away and with a strange epidemic that is feeding on the flesh of small children. It seems clear that we are dealing with a local rural situation, especially with the people's interpretation of their predicament. The gods of the land, so it is said, are angry and they seek a penance for their injunctions that have been flagrantly violated over a long period of time. Presently, Biokun steps forward. With an earthen pot and a white wrapper round his waist, the chosen carrier seems ready to undertake the rites of appeasement on behalf of the community.

But, as we should know, flood is a characteristic problem of disarticulated urbanization resulting from lack of planning and inefficient system of drainage. Actually, Elusu, the particular goddess in this regard has confessed this earlier on in the prologue and has clearly indicated her great dread of modernity. Says she to Olokun; her husband:

> Olokun; I am surprised at you. When we burst out from the bleeding gash of our mother Yemoja, were we not told to guard them jealously or else wither and die? You've been away but see, look at my face! See what the human beings have made of me, a cesspit of rotten flotsam! See how they choke my breath with oil, my belly with cement! And shit-

[11] *Esu and the Vagabond Minstrels*, though published in 1993, was first staged in 1983 at the Ekenwan campus of the University of Benin as a workshop production for Theatre Arts students.

I, Olokunsu, women of clear eyes, I have become their chamberpot! They've turned my bosom into a restless market of smugglers and pimps and murderers. Am I a whorehouse? So what has happened to the age – long injunction that they must honour my beauty and not fish in me? That they should propitiate me with sweet smelling food? Olokun, these are little tokens of respect for your wife. But see, see how they've stabbed me all over with stakes, and entangled my limbs in their fishing nets. [12]

Clearly, this community has put several thousand kilometres between itself and the traditional past. The evidence above confronts us with the ambiguities and contradictions of modernity. The discovery of oil implies wealth for the community just as cement means good houses and strong and lasting bridges. But on the flip side of these positive developments, are the reality of crimes and chaos, and the examples cited for us in this regard include smuggling and assassinations. The people have lost their innocence and have become very daring. And this is to the extent that even a goddess feels frightened by it. Seeing that death could be imminent for her should the people be allowed to so continue, Elusu decides to restore them to the old ways, the characteristics of which include fear and superstition.

But Osofisan's purpose in crafting *No more the Wasted Breed* is to prevent this backward slip. As is well known, the play is conceived as a write-back to Soyinka's *The Strong Breed*. The latter play articulates the story of a young man, Emma, who was born into a family of ritual carriers but who decides to evade that burden. Emma's strategy is to escape from home and seek solitude in a strange land. Much against himself however, the poor man finds himself running to fulfill that same responsibility in his place of exile. As he moves wobbly but inexorably to his doom, Emma recalls his father's original words of warning: "Your own blood will betray you son because you cannot hold it back." [13]

Osofisan feels angry that Soyinka could decide to sacrifice such a brilliant young man as Emma on the altar of an anachronistic practice. As he asks directly, why should anybody think of placating a god who looked on even as white predators invaded his domain and carted his people away into slavery; who would still not act when the plunderers returned with guns, seized control of the land and consequently took over the most precious of the resources of the place? Why should a people not abandon a god who rewarded dedication with betrayal? Biokun, Emma's alter ego in *No more the Wasted Breed* recovers just in time to address these and several other questions to both Elusu and Olokun:

12 Femi Osofisan, *No More the Wasted Breed* in *Morountodun and other Plays* (Ikeja: Longman, 1982): 89

13 Wole Soyinka, *The Strong Breed* in *Wole Soyinka: Collected Plays* (Oxford University Press, 1973), 134

> You watch and let them pass, these alien ships laden with plunder, with our oil and gold and diamonds, with timber, coffee, cotton and cocoa and what else.
>
> Leaving us with our hands empty. Leaving us abject and wretched, except of course, for the few traitors among us who are prosperous because they agree to serve as the agents of the white predators. Those are your friends, the ones you protect. They can go and come as they will across your waters, or across the skies of your brother Orun. You ask no sacrifice of them, no token of allegiance. They're rich and few, they are the beloved of your priest. But we're numerous and nameless, like the sand of the beach, we're wretched and expendable. A wasted breed, we're ready at a signal, to forsake our deepest dreams and take out a canoe in savage weather. We'll give our life, our blood, while they the privileged, remain here on the shore, bowing to their white masters, gathering fat... [14]

Forward then with modernity, Osofisan seems to have suggested. The gods clearly have not demonstrated any concern for what happens to the masses of the people. Like members of the class of the emergent bourgeoisie, they seem in league with capitalist powers on the other side of the Atlantic which incorporated the indigenous societies in order for them to be able to exploit the raw material production. To put the blame of the demise of traditional structures on a people who themselves have suffered unfair neglect can be likened to putting the responsibility of hacking down a tree on the handle of the axe. But what do we do about the contradictions of the emergent societies? What do we do about the picture of inequality and dislocation so graphically painted in the above quoted words of Osofisan, and which appears to be the logic of urban development in the Third World? As the playwright seems to suggest, the people themselves will need to take control of their own lives, insist on their freedom and rights, and consequently work together to create a new world. It is in an attempt to make this point that Osofisan establishes a confrontation between Elusu, the goddess of the creeks on the one hand, and Biokun and Saluga being the representatives of the new generation of humanity, on the other. But by investing the responsibility of mediation in Olokun, Osofisan, in my view, also ends up contradicting himself. Because even though he is of justice, Olokun still remains a god. The implication here is that the freedom being celebrated at the end of the play is one that has been granted by a supernatural being. It is Olokun who, having received humanity's testimony, takes a decision that Elusu is wrong and that she must die. What if he had decided otherwise? What if he had taken the path of self-preservation? And, added to this is the fact that, in the end, Olokun himself does not die; he only withdraws to the waves. "Goodbye, my love", he says as Elusu dies, *"till the next generation"* (my emphasis). [15] The underlined words give us a feeling of foreboding. The gods clearly have not died. They lie in wait on the road to the future.

---

14 *Morountodun and other Plays*, 110

15 *Morountodun and other Plays*, 110

But perhaps, Osofisan deliberately sets this contradiction so he may continue the process of resolution in *Esu and the Vagabond Minstrels*. This latter play is set at the crossroads, the homing ground of Esu, the Yoruba god of indeterminacy. The story is a simple morality tale, fetched and adapted from the repertoire of Yoruba folklore. Directly, it explores the subject of compassion, a theme that the playwright finds appropriate as he sets out with a determination to confront the crimes and brutalities of contemporary cities. Omele, one of the five vagabond musicians returns to his village after five years to discover that "development" and "civilization" have caught up with the people, and that the concept of kindness has gone out of fashion. Bewildered, he laments as he explains the new situation to fellow vagabond colleagues:

> Charity! That was the creed we were all raised on, and the whole village practised it! Not even a stranger passed by without finding a roof, or a warm bed. They taught us to always give, freely, like Mother Nature. They said God owned everything, and that every man was a creature of God. Created in his image. So how was I to know that in just five years since I left, all that would have changed? How could I have foreseen it, that a day would come when these people, my own people, would see men in torment, and drive them back into the wind? [16]

Osofisan finds justification for this new development in the orientation of the new lords of the city. These new lords are the same as the indigenous bourgeoisie which Biokun succinctly describes in *No more the Wasted Breed*: the people who plead austerity and shortages before the citizenry but open the back door for aliens to plunder the resources of their land. Rich and prosperous, they tie dogs to their door posts such that any destitutes that try to move too close to them could be torn to shreds. In the face of such blatant acts of inhumanity, it seems inevitable for people's psychic orientation to undergo some transformation.

In *Esu*, Osofisan articulates this crisis of dislocation in terms of an opposition between vice and virtue, between kindness and villainy. According to Esu, the character in the play who first appears disguised as an old man, "The owner of the world/has created a balance between the forces of good/And those of Evil. But everywhere, Evil is in the ascendant". [17] The vagabond musicians themselves have just been proscribed by the new military government and have thus had to wonder from place to place. They arrive at the crossroads tired and hungry. Collectively, they themselves are physical embodiments of this overwhelming disorientation. Their proscription is as a result of their shameless pandering to the discredited politicians while the latter were still in power. They come to the homing ground, hoping to help themselves to the offerings being made to Esu. As he appears on

[16] Femi Osofisan, *Esu and the Vagabond Minstrels* (Ibadan: New Horn Press, 1991): 7

[17] Osofisan, *Esu and the Vagabond Minstrels*, 17

stage to grant them a magic boon, Old Man asks whether they are ready "To help those among you, who are in distress? To bring redress to the wronged?/And justice to the exploited?" [18]

Of course, the vagabonds' answers were in the affirmative. But so total and so pervasive is the moral dislocation of contemporary times that the spectator knows right away that the musicians could not be taken by their pledge to abide by the injunctions. In the end, four of them misuse the power, employing it for personal enrichment. Only Omele dares to differ, demanding no material rewards from those he decides to render assistance to. But by using the power more than once, Omele also ends up violating the injunctions. He contracts leprosy and is ostracized by his colleagues. The stage instruction in part four of the play articulates a frightful contrast between Omele's condition and those of the other four minstrels. It is the same situation the following morning, according to Osofisan, and "On one side, the four lucky singers, eating and drinking merrily, all finely dressed. On the other side, alone, the leprosy-infested Omele, driving flies off his body." [19]

They are not satisfied yet, the lucky four, as we are soon to see. They heckle and jeer at Omele, pelt him with stones and would not listen to his cry of pain. They keep on assailing him until he turns finally and flees. I bring down once more the picture of the original community as drawn by Omele himself:

> Charity! That was the creed we were all raised on, and the whole village practised it! Not even a stranger passed by without finding a roof, or a warm bed. They taught us to always give, freely, like Mother Nature. They said God owned everything, and that every man was a creature of God... [20]

The society has certainly come a long way with the moral worldview of the people completely altered. So wicked have they become now and Omele has twice found himself as a victim of this collective crisis of dislocation.

As he says in the introductory note to the play, Osofisan deliberately employs this blatant sentimentalism as a means of returning (wo)man to his/her humanity. Indeed, and as he says, there is no other way to "counter today's macho world of tough American gangsters, super-bands and superman, and Kung-fu experts" [21] beside a return to primal times! Thus Osofisan follows the logic of morality tales to its very end. Old Man returns to take account of how the boon has been utilized. It turns out that the other men have only fallen for Esu's mischief. Omele, on the other hand, and through his incredible display of compassion has revealed him-

[18] Osofisan, *Esu and the Vagabond Minstrels*, 18

[19] Osofisan, *Esu and the Vagabond Minstrels*, 55

[20] Osofisan, *Esu and the Vagabond Minstrels*, 7

[21] Osofisan, *Esu and the Vagabond Minstrels*, iv

self as a child of Orunmila, the Yoruba god of divination, kindness and fellow – feeling. He is appropriately rewarded while the leprosy he earlier contracted is transferred to his colleagues.

*Esu and the Vagabond Minstrels* is Osofisan's statement on man's capacity for love and fellow-feeling, for tenderness and care even in the face of urban brutality and violence. Expectedly, the playwright soon strips his characters of their supernatural endowment. "Let the gods disappear" says the male leper, who actually is Orunmila, "to where…(they) came from/In a fairy tale." [22] Linking us concretely now with reality, Osofisan makes it clear that the riddles of evil pervading our cities have no magic solution and that goodness cannot be realized through wish fulfillments. The players themselves articulate the necessities for social and political action as they re-assemble on stage:

> JIGI….prayers are not sufficient to counter the violence in the street.
> EPO OYINBO: Neither prayers nor good wishes.
> REDIO: But only the actions of struggling men…
> EPO OYINBO: Only many fists waving together…
> REDIO: For only the muscles behind a wheel can turn it.
> JIGI: Only many voices rising together, to shout "NO", this moment…
> SIN SIN: "YES", another moment…
> EPO OYINBO: And "LET US MARCH", all the moments. [23]

There appears to be two mutually contradictory positions in this play. The main parable advocates tenderness and goodwill even in the face of utter mischief and cruelty. Omele, like a true disciple of Jesus Christ is a willing forgiver of wrongs and of acts of injustice and inhumanity. Even when his colleagues willfully conspire to chase away the woman he has liberated of a nine year-old pregnancy, Omele would still not lift up his hand. "Nothing", he answers in response to Old Man's question as to how he intends to react. After all, he continues, "They were once my comrades. They taught me all I know…I am part of them." [24]

This is outright stupidity, in my view. Certainly, human beings have to learn to combat oppression, fight injustice and resist exploitation by the force of their own arms. To acquiesce to blatant aggression as Omele has done is to encourage the perpetuation of evil. And, to be sure, what we have in *Esu…* runs against the grain of Osofisan's otherwise well-articulated vision. A self-knowledge of this contradiction on the part of the playwright perhaps explains the final, winding-up

22 Osofisan, *Esu and the Vagabond Minstrels*, 69
23 Osofisan, *Esu and the Vagabond Minstrels*, 70
24 Osofisan, *Esu and the Vagabond Minstrels*, 65

comments of his players.

The crossroads, by way of summing up on this play therefore, is a richly metaphorical location in the world of the Yorubas. It is the point of destiny, of transformation. For the inhabitants of a typical African city that developed as a consequence of total displacement, complete disorientation and acute dislocation, the person to position in such a place is surely not Omele. Neither can it be any of the four minstrels. The person that suits that place may be found in *No More the Wasted Breed,* the first play discussed in this essay. Saluga is measured and humane; he is unflinching in solidarity and commitment, just as he is unbending of will and unshakeable in principle. Inhabitants of contemporary African, nay Third World, cities need these qualities.

This essay commences by underlining the tensions characterizing the modern city in general. It then proceeds to point out the marginal position of Third World cities; its peculiarly unfair and degrading condition and how this has engaged the attention of different writers. Ultimately, I establish Africa as my focus and picked out Femi Osofisan for illustration. In the discussion of *No More the Wasted Breed* and *Esu and the Vagabond Minstrels*- being the two plays used as examples- I foreground the playwright's peculiar approach to city dislocations: how he employs local traditions and images even as he engages contemporary urban problems. But, as the analysis has hopefully shown, the transformative alternative negotiated by the playwright in both works is fraught with ambiguities.

## WORKS CITED

Clark, J.P. 'Ibadan,' in *Poems of Black Africa* (ed.) Wole Soyinka (London: Heinemanns, 1975): 142

Gilbert, Alan & Josef Gugler. *Cities, Poverty and Development: Urbanization in the Third World* (New York: Oxford University Press, 1975)

Gilbert, Alan. 'Urban Development in a World System,' in *Cities, Poverty and Development: Urbanization in the Third World* ed. Michael P. Weber & Anne Lloyd (New York: Oxford University Press, 1975)

Osofisan, Femi. *No More the Wasted Breed* in *Moroundodun and other Plays* (Ikeja: Longmans, 1982)

Osofisan, Femi. *Once Upon Four Robbers* (Ibadan: Heinemann Books, 1991)

Sandberg, Carl. *Chicago Poems* (New York: Atheneum, 1963)

Soyinka, Wole. *Collected Plays* (Oxford: Oxford University Press, 1973)

Wa Thiong'o, Ngugi. *A Grain of Wheat* (London: Heinemanns, 1967)

Wa Thiong'o, Ngugi. *Petals of Blood* (London: Heinemanns, 1977)

Weber P. Michael & Anne Lloyd. *The American City* (St. Paul West Publishing Co, 1975

# Part II

# The cultural, the political…

# CHAPTER 8

# OIL RESOURCES, HEGEMONIC POLITICS AND THE STRUGGLE FOR RE-INVENTING POSTCOLONIAL NIGERIA[1]

I am recreating the Ogoni people; first and foremost, to come to the realization of what they have always been which British colonization tried to take away from them. So my effort is very intellectual. It is backed by theories, thoughts and ideas, which will, in fact, matter to the rest of Africa in the course of time.[2]

The citation above puts in perspective the different dimensions of the protests and struggles inspired and led by Ken Saro-Wiwa, the former president of the Association of Nigerian Authors (ANA) and Movement for the Survival of Ogoni peoples (MOSOP). Indeed, of the different forms of agitations against neglect and environmental degradation put forward, to date, by the different communities of the oil-producing areas, that of the Ogonis remains the most rigorously planned, the most well-articulated and the most sustained.[3]

Since its discovery in commercial quantities in the country in 1956, oil has steadily displaced agriculture as Nigeria's prime source of foreign exchange earnings. When Shell D'Arcy, the Anglo-Dutch Petroleum Corporation, which later transformed to Shell Petroleum Development Company, shipped out the first 5,000 barrels in 1958, the price of crude oil was only four US dollars per barrel. But by 1981, when more than fifteen oil companies jointly extracted over two million barrels daily from the innumerable oil wells strewn all over the Niger Delta, the price per barrel had risen to 40 dollars. And even when in the 1990s the

1 An earlier version of this chapter was first published in *Ogoni's Agonies: Ken Saro – Wiwa and the Crisis in Nigeria*, ed. AbdulRasheed Na'Allah (Trenton, NJ: Africa World Press, 1998): 98 – 101

2 Ken Saro – Wiwa, "They are Killing my People." Interview in *The News* (May 17, 1993): 44

3 This statement was originally made in 1998. Since then, several other movements have risen up in the Niger Delta region of Nigeria agitating for, among others, resource control, fiscal federalism and a re-dressing of environmental pollution. The strategies adopted by these new groups are far more militant than that of the one led by Ken Saro – Wiwa, and it will not amount to any exaggeration to describe the crisis in the region now as one of emergency proportion. Even then, the agitation sponsored by the Ogonis still stands among the best planned and the most selflessly prosecuted.

production fell by about 40 percent and the price came down to only a little over $16.00 US dollars, oil still accounted for over 95 percent of the nation's yearly expenditure. [4]

Paradoxically, the same resource representing the power-house of national life also serves as a big agency of dislocation and disorientation for the several million people inhabiting the areas where it is produced. Directly, the dislocation and disorientation derive from two complementary and inter-related factors: the first being the devastating impact of the exploration of the resources on the environment, and the second that of the cruel neglect of the people of the area by successive Nigerian administrations.

Claude Ake, the late respected Director of the Port Harcourt-based Centre for Advanced Social Sciences (CASS), analysed the first factor in highly scientific and technical terms in his article, "Shelling Nigeria Ablaze," [5] published in the *Tell* magazine edition of January 29, 1996. According to him, Nigeria flares at least 76 percent of the total natural gas derived from petroleum production. At temperatures, in his own words, "of 1,300 to 1.400 degree centigrade, the multitude of flares in the Delta heat up everything causing noise pollution and producing $SO_2$, Voc, carbon dioxide and Nox and particulates around the clock." [6] Arguing further, Ake contends that with 35 million tons of carbon dioxide and 12 million tons of methane released every year from the flaring "Nigerian oil fields contribute more in global warming than the rest of the world put together" [7]. On oil spills, the Nigerian National Merit Award Winner reveals that the States of Rivers, Bayelsa and Delta as the principal oil producing areas in Nigeria experience about "300 major oil spills a year ... which discharge about 2,300$m^3$ of oil," [8] As Ake insists, the above analysis fails to take into reckoning the "minor spills which are far more numerous and (which are) invariably under-reported," Ake writes further on effluents, the treatment of which no single oil company in Nigeria has bothered to take interest in:

> According to an European Community study, *Mangroves of Africa and Madagascar*, the waters of the Niger Delta contain at least 8 [parts per million] of petroleum and often up to 60 [parts per million]. An environmental impact study of Shell *(Designer Industries*, 1993) put an average hydrocarbon content of petroleum hydrocarbons in wastewater in Oloma creek at 62.7 mg/I. At the Bonny Terminal in Rivers State where Shell does its

4 Today, due to the dimension that the Iraq war has taken, the oil prices has soared very high and the price is now almost $145 per barrel. The product still remains the mainstay of Nigeria's economy.

5 Claude Ake, "Shelling Nigeria Ablaze." Interview in *Tell* (January 29, 1996): 37–42

6 Claude Ake, 40

7 Ake, 40

8 Ake, 40

separation of water from crude oil, the mud at the bottom of the Bonny River has a lethal concentration of 12,000 pm. But Shell lies that the wastewater at Bonny Terminal averages 7.8 mg/I. As the World Bank report quoted above has noted, the industry is using API separator and TPF basin facilities, which are unsuitable for separation of better than 50mg/I performance.[9]

To understand the practical import of the above analysis, I turn first to a *Newswatch* report of 1985[10]. The report paints a graphic picture of the terrible hazards suffered by the people of Iko, a small community in Ikot Abasi local government area of Cross River State from which Shell has explored oil since 1973. According to the news magazine, the white, salty vapour fired into the air in the process of separating gas from oil causes corrosion and perforation on the roofs of the buildings of the villagers. The same vapour, when it settles on the skin turns it into a "charred surface in the form of an unsightly skin disease."[11] As the report further states, an 18 year old boy who fell victim of this disease could not be properly treated because Iko has no single health centre or clinic. In addition, there is also the effect of consistent explosions which causes many of the buildings to shake and the walls to crack. Because of this, many of the villagers have had to abandon their houses, migrating to other villages in search of refuge.

As the same *Newswatch* report shows, the combined effects of oil spills, chemical spills and gas flaring have devastated the lands and polluted the rivers of Mgbede/Ebocha/Omiku of, this time, Ahoada local government area of Rivers State. Indeed, as a result of this pollution, several schools of fish have had to flee and this has made fishing, the traditional occupation of the people, to become sheer indulgence. And the same goes for farming. In fact, as Akinrinade further points out, a completely burnt down area of about 1.5 km circumference represents an evidence of the kind of disaster that certain chemicals can wreck on plants.[12]

The story is not in any way different in Ogoniland which is located in the North-Eastern part of the Delta region. "Ogoni suffered and continues to suffer the degrading effects of oil exploration and exploitation," says G.B. Leton, founding president of the Movement for the Survival of the Ogoni People (MOSOP). In the statement published as an introduction to *Ogoni Bill Of Rights* issued in 1992, Leton successfully confronts the world with the hazardous consequences of environmental despoliation and chemical contamination. He writes:

> Lands, streams and creeks are totally and continually polluted; the atmosphere is forever charged with hydrocarbons, carbon monoxide and carbon dioxide; many villages experi-

---

9 Ake, 40

10 Soji Akinrinade, "Paradox of Oil Areas." In *Newswatch*, (December 23, 1985): 29 – 35

11 Akinrinade, 33

12 Akinrinade, 33

ence the infernal quaking of the wrath of gas flares which have been burning 24 hours a day for 33 years; acid rain, oil spillages and blow-outs are common. The results of such unchecked environmental pollution and degradation are that: (i) the Ogoni can no longer farm successfully. Once the food basket of the Eastern Niger Delta, the Ogoni now buy food (when they can afford it) (ii) Fish, once a common source of protein, is now rare. Owing to the constant and continual pollution of our streams and creeks, fish can only be caught in deeper and offshore waters for which the Ogoni are not equipped (iii) All wildlife is dead (iv) The ecology is changing fast. The mangrove tree, the aerial roots of which (sic) normally provide a natural and welcome habitat for many a sea food – crabs, periwinkles, mud skippers, cockles, mussels, shrimps and all – is now being gradually replaced by unknown and otherwise useless palms. (v) The health hazards generated by an atmosphere charged with hydrocarbon vapour, carbon monoxide and carbon dioxide are innumerable.[13]

Let me, at this point, return quickly to an earlier point I made to the effect that the two causative factors of dislocation and disorientation suffered by the people of oil-producing areas are closely inter-connected. Certainly, there is no other way to capture a situation where successive administrations remain unmoved even as these people experience incalculable damages as a result of environmental degradation and abuse if not as criminal neglect. Anyhow, there is a basic sense of the word which refers to circumstances of absolute absence of infrastructural facilities like roads, water, light, health care system and schools. And, as incredible as these may seem, this is the situation with most oil – bearing communities in Nigeria.

Approaching this argument, I take inspiration from the words of Dr. Dappa Biriye, Niger Delta's sole delegate to the constitutional debates in London during the pre-independence era. Biriye makes it clear in a December 1990 interview with *African Concord*[14] that to fully comprehend the present state of deprivation of oil communities in Nigeria, it may be necessary to adopt Oloibiri, their forerunner as a pattern.

Coming to Oloibiri for the first time in 1956, the white oil explorers had brought along with them their own 'pre-fabricated houses'[15] which served for temporary accommodation while *Shell Oloibiri*, their new quarters were being constructed. On completion, the new city immediately took over as the commercial nerve-centre of the ancient town. Inevitably, or so it would seem, indigenes of the community also trooped to the new estate to take up employment as gardeners, cooks, messengers, cleaners and house-helps. Beside this labour exploitation, Shell staff made sure that they had no other form of contact with the indigenous

---

13 G.B. Leton, "Introduction," *Ogoni Bill of Rights* (Port Harcourt: Saros International Publishers, 1992): 6–7

14 Demola Abimboye, "Massacre at Dawn." *African Concord* (December 3, 1990): 23–31

15 *African Concord*, 25

people of Oloibiri. Whatever was needed and which could not be acquired from the new market, was ferried in from Port Harcourt. The result today is that after oil resources worth several billions of dollars had been exploited from the bowels of Oloibiri, the town now stands in 'limbo,' totally and completely abandoned as it were. It has no roads, no electricity, no drinking water, no telephone facilities, no postal agency and no good school or any well-equipped health care centre. *African Concord* quotes M.O. Egba, a member of the community's Council of Chiefs as having said that the story of Oloibiri could be likened to that "of a crawling snail picked up by a hunter who (simply) took out the meat inside, and threw the shell carelessly away." [16]

Oloibiri certainly provides the pattern. Because the story is the same in many other places: in Umuechem, in Oboburu, and in Ogoni – all of Rivers State; in Qua Iboe, Akwa Ibom State; in Obokofia and Obiakpo, Delta State; and in a hundred other communities of the Niger Delta where several barrels of oil are exploited daily.

The same story of stagnation and bare-faced injustice persists everywhere. To cite just one more example, Escravos is an offshore community located in Delta State. For the indigenous people of this area, time has stood still for several decades. The village is completely inaccessible by road. There is drinking water, but no medical facility and no reliable power supply system. Yet, to the other side of this community live about two hundred staff members of Gulf Oil Company. Akinrinade writes of the residential quarters in the same *Newswatch* edition of December 23, 1985:

> The housing estate, otherwise called a tank farm, is a Hollywood kind of layout. Well-nurtured lawns, beautiful streets, uninterrupted electricity and ever-flowing pipe-borne water are what the oilmen enjoy. Recreational facilities like lawn tennis courts, bowling alleys, snooker and tennis tables are in abundance. There is a cinema hall that opens at 8 pm everyday for the 200 workers that live on the farm. (Indeed), for them life is full of roses after a hard day's job on the oil rigs. [17]

To be sure, it is not as if the people of the different indigenous communities have themselves always remained passive in the face of acute contradictions and oppressive control. In fact, the words of Saro-Wiwa presented as an epigram at the beginning of this essay are located in the context of the minority rights activist's attempt at delineating the point of departure between the struggles of his own people and the one of the mid-1960s prosecuted by Isaac Adaka Boro, arguably the forerunner in the agitations against neglect and environmental despoliation in the Niger Delta.

[16] *African Concord*, 1990, 29
[17] Akinrinade, Soji, 17

Standing at the head of an ill-equipped but highly determined group of soldiers, Boro had, in 1966, unilaterally declared the Republic of Niger Delta in what, as G.G. Darah states in *The Guardian* on Sunday of November 19, 1995, is now known as a "12-day revolution." Determined "to demonstrate to the world what and how we feel about oppression," [18] Boro's army had overrun the Ijaw territory, receiving great accolades and ovations from the people of the area. Eventually overpowered by the federal troops, Boro was convicted for treason and consequently condemned to death. He was however a little lucky in the sense that he escaped the hangman's noose via a state pardon he received in August 1966. He was to die a few months later fighting on the federal side during the Nigerian civil war. Saro-Wiwa was not particularly impressed by Boro's efforts. To the Ogoni leader, it was actually no more than "a quixotic experiment, which bemused his people." [19]

After Boro, oil installation blockades became the major mode of articulated resistance against dislocation in the oil producing region of Nigeria. Shell, the leading oil company in the country experienced at least twenty – two of such blockades within the first eight months of that particular year. [20] Also citing from a paper presented by Bola Adewale, a law lecturer at the Institute of Advanced Legal Studies, University of Lagos during a seminar organized for top officers of oil companies, the same edition of *Newswatch* reveals that three hundred and forty – four of such blockades were officially recorded between 1976 and 1988 and that in over two hundred of such cases, real damages were done to the flow-pipes. A typical example of such blockades was prosecuted by the people of Kolo creeks, Brass local government area of Rivers State in July, 1990. Directly, the people of Imiringi, Elebele and Otuesega, three of the communities in the area had invaded the oil installations, took over the control room and locked up the staff on duty. They also took over the helipad and successfully prevented Shell's intervention team from landing. Eventually, the company had to seek help from the police and the army but the villagers held on, threatening "to blow-up the installations if any of them sustained any injuries from the police." [21] After a week of the face-off, an agreement was reached which committed Shell to some construction projects in the area.

Palliative measures that hardly scratch the surface of things, but that agreement is a typical programme of oil-producing companies in their terrains of operation. A few scholarships to some secondary school or university students, provision of drinking water via bore-holes or taps, electricity supply projects, dona-

[18] G.G. Darah, "Dying for the Niger Delta"' in *The Guardian* (November 19, 1995): B1 – 3

[19] *The News*, 23

[20] Soji Akinrinade, "Killing the Geese." *Newswatch* (October 15, 1990): 32 – 36

[21] Soji Akinrinade, 1990, 33

tions to community schools, road construction, reconstruction or rehabilitation, agricultural and fishing projects are representative of some of the community development programmes of oil companies as they struggle to contain the inevitable tensions generated in different areas of the Niger Delta. The projects are scattered and staggered all over the oil-producing communities and, therefore, are hardly of any impact. Even then, this is when the indigenous people are lucky. At other times, the affected company simply drafts in the police once they find themselves confronted with hostilities by their hosts. And when such happens, the consequences are often tragic for the local communities.

Such is the fate of the people of Umuechem; a small oil town located North West of Port Harcourt. It was on October 31, 1990 when the people of the community assembled in the town square to mount a peaceful protest against their continual dislocation. Unknown to the villagers, Shell officials, afraid of the possible damages the people might do to their facilities had simply sent for the police as soon as they sensed trouble. The mobile team arrived to open fire on the unsuspecting people who instinctively decided to fight back. The ensuing clash led to the beheading of a policeman who himself had shot dead one of the villagers. The police consequently withdrew to re-mobilize. The ultimate confrontation led to the death of over 85 people including the traditional chief of the town and two of his grown – up sons. In addition, the police set ablaze not only the houses in the town but also its two churches, the only community primary school and the health care centre. *African Concord* reports as follows on the incident:

> The team forcefully occupied Umuechem for six days; 1 to 6 November. During the week-long siege, the policemen fed on goats, chickens, sheep and pigs. They made a home of the beer parlour in the community, while economic trees such as coconut, and citrus were cut down for food. "It was a revolt against a quiet community, a war in its entirety" commented an eye-witness. [22]

It was against this background that the Ogonis embarked on their own struggles in early 1990. The first thing they did at the start was to draft the *Bill of Rights,* earlier referred to, and which articulated in intellectual terms the basis and justification for their struggle. Signed by the representatives of the Six Ogoni Kingdoms on August 26, 1990 and based on Awolowo's proposal in *Thoughts on Nigerian Constitution* that all ethnic groups in Nigeria, no matter the size, be accorded equal treatment in the federal system which in theory operates in the country, the *Ogoni Bill of Rights* has far-reaching implications for the Nigerian constitution. The bill demands ethnic autonomy and self-determination for the people of Ogoniland. By ethnic autonomy is meant, and in the words of Ken Saro-Wiwa in a foreword to the bill, "political control of Ogoni affairs by Ogoni people, control and use of

[22] *African Concord,* 25

Ogoni economic resources for Ogoni development, adequate and direct representations and the right to protect the Ogoni environment and ecology from further degradation."[23] An added dimension of the declaration was a demand for 20 billion U.S. dollars quoted as royalties and rents "for petroleum mined from our soil for over 33 years."[24]

The document was officially addressed to General Ibrahim Babangida, then the country's military president, and members of his Armed Forces Ruling Council (AFRC) on October 2, 1990. Having waited for one year without any response whatsoever from the government, an addendum mandates the Movement for the Survival of the Ogoni People (MOSOP) to make representations to relevant international bodies with a view to getting them to prevail on the Nigerian government to respond to the demands in the bill. Thus began an intense campaign which took Saro-Wiwa before such international organizations as the Ethnic Minority Rights Organisation of Africa (EMIROAF), the Unrepresented Nations and People's Organisation (UNPO) and the United Nation's Sub-Commission of Human Rights on the Prevention of Discrimination (against), and Protection of the Minorities. Partly to complement the above efforts and partly as well to keep up the level of awareness, a variety of activities were organized in the home-front. These included rallies, mass protests and demonstrations, award ceremonies, commemorations of important dates, vigils, blockades and media campaigns. So successful were these activities that for the Nigerian ruling elite to have continued to look on would have meant for it to have sanctioned its own perils. This exactly is the meaning of Ogoni tragedy.

If I insist that the struggle of the Ogoni people represents the most well-articulated and the best prosecuted of all of the efforts articulated against hegemonic exploitation in the Niger Delta, it is not because of a wholesale approval of the method of, and the vision propelling, the agitations. Saro-Wiwa, arguing that after over thirty years of absolute control of power, the leadership of the majority ethnic groups in Nigeria has shown itself to be inept, corrupt and incompetent proposes a fundamental transformation of the Nigerian structure, which transformation will invest in each ethnic group the control of both its political and economic resources. "I am rallying for ethnic autonomy, resolve and environmental control" says he in *Tell*, February 8, 1993. "The only law to be in Nigeria is: You are free to rule yourself, you're independent now, but you must pay your bills, you will control your resources, you control your environment, run whatever government you like."[25]

---

23 *Ogoni Bill or Rights*, (Port Harcourt: Saros International Publishers, 1992): 2

24 *Bill of Rights*, 23

25 *Tell*, 1993: 32

As well articulated as it is, the perspective put forward by Saro-Wiwa is fraught with a number of important pitfalls. For one, in advocating ethnic autonomy, it does not seem to occur to the well – known leader of the Ogoni people that it is possible for the leadership of any of the resulting nationalities to be hijacked by opportunists and self-seeking people who, inevitably, will go ahead to foist their own form of hegemonic control and domination on the people and eventually continue the oppression. Saro-Wiwa also perceives the Hausa-Fulani as that ethnic group which dominates the nation's political landscape and which exploits her resources. This, to some extent, may not be untrue, especially if one considers the influential position of the caliphate and the fact that of a total of nearly forty eight years of the country's independence, the group alone has produced eight out of the country's thirteen heads of state and these together have ruled for a total of twenty – six years (five and a half years of Tafawa Balewa, six months of Murtala Muhammed, four years of Shagari, fourteen of Buhari-Babangida-Abacha interregnum, one of Abdulsalami Abubakar and a year and a half so far of Umar Yaradua). Even as this is the situation however, it is also the case that the common Hausa-Fulani, comprehensively in terms of material condition and available opportunities stands, arguably, among the most hopeless and wretched in contemporary Nigeria. The point here, simply, is that this man or woman – the common Hausa-Fulani man or woman that is – may as much be a victim of hegemonic conspiracy as is the Ogoni man or woman.

Since I do not want to be misunderstood, let it be stated categorically that the Nigerian problem has a clear nationality dimension to it. Jibril Aminu, in 1990 contends that the Niger Delta region remains undeveloped because of its "very harsh" terrain. "Transportation is difficult", he says, "because the creeks are difficult." [26] Aminu was Nigeria's former oil minister and this statement was made by him thirty – two clear years after oil exploration first commenced in the country. Because of this, it is important to ask the man whether the areas, in any way, are more difficult than, say, Lagos or even Abuja. The former as the erstwhile capital city of Nigeria, in spite of its many creeks, its marshes and swamps and even the lagoon and the Atlantic Ocean can, guardedly, be described as having a fine network of roads. The latter, the current capital city was – still is – a very hilly terrain, and largely a virgin expanse of land which was opened up and built from the scratch.

But the argument cannot stop here, no. Because, while successive governments in the same Lagos expend several billions of naira to contain ocean surge in Victoria Island on a yearly basis, the slums of Ajegunle and the ghettoes of Mushin remain unattended to. And while the city of Abuja is beautiful, indeed

---

[26] Soji Akinrinade, 1990: 35

very beautiful, it serves as homes only to the few, very highly – placed members of the society. The teeming masses of people who are engaged, one way or the other in the city, are not at all provided for by the authorities. They actually travel in on a daily basis from the adjoining villages and hamlets where they actually lead a sub – human existence.

Yes, the Niger Delta terrain is difficult, very difficult: but how come it was possible for Gulf Oil to erect a tank farm in Escravos and Forcados?

So what point am I trying to make here? It is simply that a comprehensive analysis of Nigerian problem will have to take into consideration the nature of the economic system in operation and, in particular, the mode of distribution of available resources. It will also have to contend with the strong alliance existing between the ruling class (military as well as civilian) and the several multinational corporations operating in the country. If closely examined, it will be revealed that it is this alliance which in the specific case of oil producing areas, makes it possible for the oil companies to simply call on the police (and the army in some instances) as soon as they perceive any security problem. Claude Ake in the same 1996 essay of his referred to earlier in this paper raises an alarm over what he describes as "the privatization of the state" [27] by Shell. By privatization of the state, Ake refers to the presence of armed troops and policemen in the residential quarters as well as the offices and operational bases of the company. He writes further:

> It is indicative of Shell's privatization of the state and its prerogatives that it buys substantial quantities of firearms through open tender for its own use. *This Day* of Friday, December 22, 1995, reports a case before a Lagos High Court in which an arms dealer, Humanities Nigeria Limited, sued Shell Nigeria for 30 million [Naira] for a breach of contract which Shell awarded in 1993. In a 17-paragraph affidavit sworn to by the chief executive of the company, Gabriel Akinluyi, the company says that Shell was making the purchase to update the firearms of its security across the country. [28]

Ake ends his piece by calling for an inquiry into the purchase and use of firearms by Shell but I think he misses the point. The way that Shell behaved during the Ogoni crises, including its vehement rejection of any blame in the matter, can only be indicative of one thing: that it enjoyed, and continues to enjoy, the full cooperation of, and protection from, the state. Now that the situation has begun to unravel and the crisis has started to assume a very frightening dimension, neither the government of Nigeria, nor Shell, nor any of the other multinational companies exploring oil in the Niger Delta seems ready to take on the problem in the appropriate way. Well, in 'Before I am Hanged', the statement he presented before the Justice Ibrahim Auta panel just four days before he faced the hangman,

27 "Shelling Nigeria Ablaze," 40
28 "Shelling Nigeria Ablaze," 40

Saro Wiwa says that he has "no doubt in my mind that the ecological war the company has waged in the Delta will be called to question sooner than later" [29]. The words are already proving prophetic not only for Shell which the executed writer specifically had in mind here, but also for other individuals and corporate bodies who have vested interests in the region.

[29] Ken Saro – Wiwa. "Before I am Hanged." (*ANA Review*, October 31, 1995): 22

## WORKS CITED

Abimboye, Demola. "Massacre at Dawn" in *African Concord.* (December 3, 1990): 23–31.

Ake, Claude. "Shelling Nigeria Ablaze" in *Tell.* (January 29, 1996): 40

Akinrinade, Soji. "Killing the Geese" in *Newswatch* (October 15, 1990): 32–36

Akinrinade, Soji. "Paradox of Oil Areas" in *Newswatch.* (December 23 1985).

Darah, G.G. "Dying for the Niger Delta" in *The Guardian on Sunday.* (November 19, 1995): B1–3.

*Ogoni Bill of Rights.* (Port Harcourt: Saros International Publishers): 1992.

Omonubi, Rolake. "Oil, Oil, Where Is Naira" in *Newswatch.* (December 5, 1987): 55–6.

Saro-Wiwa, Ken. "Before I Am Hanged" in *ANA Review.* (November 1995): 13.

– "They Are Killing My People". Interview. *The News.* (May 17, 1993): 22–7

– "We Will Defend Our Oil with Blood". Interview. *Tell.* (February 8, 1993): 28–33

# CHAPTER 9

# INSIDE AFRICA: NOTES ON BAYREUTH AFRICAN STUDIES SERIES[1]

## I

The first edition of the Bayreuth African Studies Series (henceforth interchangeably used with its acronym, BASS) was published in 1984. It was a modest 85-page monograph with the cover boldly announcing, in addition to the title of the series, the theme of the edition: "The Sudan: Ethnicity and National Cohesion." The flip page of the front cover also announced Eckhard Breitinger and Reinhard Sanders as publishers/editors, giving their joint address as Bayreuth University, West Germany – Germany at that time was still split into two.

There was also a terse note from the editors stating that the series was being "published in cooperation with the special research project 'Identity in Africa' (SFB 2014) of the German Research Council (DFG) and the Africa Area Studies Programme of the University of Bayreuth."[2] Altogether, there were three titles in the edition. The first one, "Ethnicity, Regionalism and National Cohesion in the Sudan," was written by Mohammed Omar Bashir; the second, contributed by Mohammed A.R. Mohammed Saleh, is titled "National vs. Regional: Some Methodological Problems in the Study of Nationalism and Nation-Building in the Sudan"; while the third, "The Dynamics of Ethnic Identification in Northern Darfur: a Situational Approach," has Musa Abdul-Jalil as the author. All three contributors are from the University of Khartoum, Sudan.

BASS set out with the objective of providing an outlet for the articulation of critical positions on different aspects of African Studies. It also professed the aim of promoting dialogues and debates between African scholars and their European and North American counterparts. Now, almost twenty – five years after it first took off, the series has been able to push out well over eighty volumes

---

1 An earlier version of this chapter was first published in *Palavers of African Literature: Essays in Honor of Bernth Lindfors, Vol. 1* Ed. Toyin Falola and Barbara Harlow. (Trenton, NJ: Africa World Press, 2002): 257 – 285

2 Eckhard Breitinger & Reinhard Sanders, *The Sudan: Ethnicity and National Cohesion.* (Bayreuth: Bayreuth African Studies Series, 1984): v

of books and monographs particularly on literature, but also on theatre, sociology, education, philosophy, music, law, women's studies, religion and languages and linguistics. In this chapter, I investigate the point of departure of Bayreuth African Studies Series as a publishing venture, review its output and explore its breakthroughs and limitations, as well as its plans and prospects for the future.

## II

It was fairly easy, giving birth to BASS. As noted earlier, Bayreuth University at that time had a huge research project on Africa which was sponsored by the German research conglomerate, the Deutsche Forschungsgemeinschaft (DFG). Titled "Identity in Africa," the project had Professor K. Rupert, who was later to become the President of the University, as its director. As a multi-disciplinary research programme then, Identity in Africa spread over a gamut of disciplines including literature, religion, sociology, law, economics, languages and linguistics, anthropology, and so on. What this meant was that scholars, researchers, and artists from Africa, and experts on different aspects of African studies were being invited to Bayreuth to give talks, deliver papers, participate in conferences and symposia, and conduct research on a short term basis. Apparently the project steering committee did not give a serious thought to the question of how to push out in published form some of the results of these wide – ranging research activities. Eckhard Breitinger and Reinhard Sanders decided to seize the initiative by starting a monograph that would specifically publish some of the proceedings of the programme. And the project committee not only very readily agreed with the idea, it also decided to buy a significant number of copies of every edition wholesale. This meant that once any issue came out of the press, a substantial sum of money would be earned almost instantly, enabling the editors to proceed on the next edition. So it went on smooth-sailing – but only at the beginning.

Because soon, Reinhard Sanders took a decision to relocate to the United States of America in search of greener pastures. Thus Breitinger found himself saddled all alone with the responsibility of keeping the flag of the monograph flying. This was after only ten editions. An even greater challenge was to come soon after Sanders' departure: the Identity in Africa project wound up just after the fifteenth edition was published. Eckhard Breitinger – whose more than twenty-year career as a teacher and researcher of the literatures of Africa and her Diaspora had taken him to the United state of America, the Caribbean, and several African countries including Nigeria, Cameroon, Uganda, and Ghana-had to sit down and think over the future of the project to which he had by now become totally committed. This happened in 1991.

Besides finance, Breitinger had a second question to tackle. And this had to do with how to make the series achieve greater respectability and impact. Respectability here has nothing to do with the quality of the content of the series or the thematic or geographical scope of the contributions. To be sure, the monograph by this time had pushed out several fresh and original articles – relatively – on different aspects of African Studies. Taken together, the first edition provides well-grounded information on the crisis in The Sudan. The second edition tackles the question of authenticity in African languages and literatures and contains an article on early twentieth-century Swahili prose narrative contributed by Jack D. Rollin of the University of Indiana, Bloomington, and another on the development of Sierra Leone Krio by Alex Johnson of the University of Sierra Leone. The third edition is on Francophone African Literature, and all three articles in it are presented in French. Josef Schmied, who had researched extensively on the English language in East Africa, contributed a chapter on the English language in Tanzania to the fifth edition and returned to edit issue no. 15, which was solely devoted to English in East and Central Africa. In the seventh edition, which focuses on Drama and Theatre in Africa, Karin Barber, a British research scholar in Yoruba language and literature based at the Centre of West African Studies, University of Birmingham, has a well-informed and highly perceptive – even if dispassionate article on Yoruba popular theatre. Akinola Aguda, the respected Nigerian legal luminary who also was at one time the Chief Judge of Botswana, appears in the eleventh edition with "The Machinery of Justice and the Training and Appointment of Judges in Nigeria." The same edition contains another paper on "The Impact of English Law Concepts on the Administration of Islamic Law in Nigeria," contributed by Abdur-Rahman Doi, a respected scholar of Islamic Legal Studies in Nigeria. The point of all this, in short, is that there is no way that a series which has attracted contributions from reputable scholars from different disciplines, different locations, and different ethnic, racial, and religious backgrounds can be described as sub-standard. It would seem, however, that Breitinger, perhaps because of his experience and rating in the field of African studies, felt dissatisfied with a cheaply produced monograph pushing out three articles per edition on the average, with severely limited circulation. And even though he had no funds, he was determined to turn the series into a more prestigious publication which could be used to carry out sustained explorations of different themes and subjects in its field of coverage, and which would, relatively speaking, circulate far and wide. Thus it happened that the monograph gradually dove-tailed into an independent book series financed mainly through sales and adverts. To date, there have been published approximately seventy volumes of books.

## III

To be sure, BASS is not another run-of-the-mill publication venture. First, as I have implied, the initial factor motivating it was more professional than commercial. Second, it has a relatively restricted focus: African Studies. Third, it betrays an intense loyalty to the factor which gave it the original impetus: the African Studies programme of Bayreuth University. Together these three factors influenced its selection procedure as well as its mode of operation. For now its output has three discernible categories. The first, which is also the largest, relates directly to the programme just mentioned. While the "Identity in Africa" programme has, indeed, wound up, the various academic and research programmes in African Studies in Bayreuth University have continued. This means that conferences and workshops have continued to be organized, that writers, artists, composers, scholars, and researchers have continued to be invited under different kinds of programmes, and for varying lengths of time, that fellowship winners and scholarship holders have continued to use the University as their research base, and that doctoral candidates have continued to turn in dissertations on various themes and subjects. In all of these situations, Breitinger has remained on high alert, forever ready, as it were, to examine the products of these wide-ranging activities and to turn out the more seminal ones for wider readership.

The second group is intimately connected with the first. As a coordinator of a research programme in African Studies, Breitinger himself has remained quite productive. He has continued to conduct researches, to carry out outreach programmes, and to organize workshops, seminars, and conferences both in Bayreuth and in selected African countries. BASS has also become a ready outlet for the product of some of these activities.

The third group comprises of occasional works submitted by independent researchers and scholars for publication. It seems a measure of the publisher cum editor's dynamism that he could decide to invest in some of these works. What follows represents a further discussion of sample publications under each of the categories.

## IV

As a visiting research scholar at the University of Bayreuth between 1986 and 1990, Akin Euba, the Nigerian Art Music composer and musicologist was charged with the responsibility of putting together an archive of modern African music for Iwalewa Haus, the Africa Centre of the University. This assignment enabled him to conduct research into a number of topics on certain aspects of intercultural music in Africa. The research produced four seminal papers first tested at different conferences and workshops held in London, Melbourne, and Bayreuth. As soon as he had finished working on the final versions of these papers, Breitinger took hold of the manuscripts, editing them by himself and quickly transforming them into Bayreuth African Studies series 16 under the title *Essays on African Music 2: Intercultural Perspectives.* [3]

Extremely huge and comprehensive as it was, the Identity in Africa programme had one great deficiency – it did not make provision for women studies. It was partly in order to compensate for this that Gudrum Ludwar-Ene and Mechthild Reh, both of whom were themselves involved in the programme, proceeded on a compilation of eight articles covering a range of themes on women in countries such as Cameroon, Zambia, Uganda, Ivory Coast, and Nigeria. *Focus on Women in Africa,* the English version of the title of what became issue number 26, was "based on... fieldwork data on the situation of women in various countries of West and East Africa." As the blurb further states, the essays in the book:

> cover a wide range of topics such as the concept of "sleeping pregnancy" (kwnatacce) as it affects Hausa women in Northern Nigeria, women as media in different cults in Uganda, gender differences in socialization in Abidjan and Cameroon, industrial entrepreneurship and urban-rural ties among women in Nigeria, the legal position of widows in Zambia and female utopias in the lyric verse of Veronique Tadjo (Ivory Coast). [4]

Issue number 44 of the Bayreuth African Studies Series titled *Blackness: Culture, Ideology and Discourse* [5] is authored by Femi Abodunrin. The man had completed a doctoral dissertation on the theme of blackness in the writings of Wole Soyinka, Derek Walcott, and Amiri Baraka at Stirling University, Scotland, in 1993. In 1995, he was awarded a one-year research fellowship by the Alexander von Humboldt Foundation, Germany. Abodunrin utilized the fellowship in Bayreuth working on, among other things, an expanded version of his dissertation. The re-worked thesis, which now included three additional authors, namely: Obotunde Ijimere and Wale Ogunyemi of Nigeria and Jorge Amado of Brazil, proposes a theory of criticism of black writings that merges the tricksterist articulation of Esu, the Yoruba god of indeterminacy, with the Bakhtinian theory of the carnivalesque. It was published in 1996.

I have stated earlier that the scope of the first group is diverse. Indeed, the African Studies programme of Bayreuth University is probably the most extensive in Europe, and Breitinger has been very effective at monitoring it. *Land Law and*

---

3 Akin Euba, *Essays on Music in Africa2: Intercultural Perspectives.* (Bayreuth: Bayreuth African Studies Series, 1989)

4 Gudrun Ludwar – Ene & Reh Mechthild ed. *Focus on Women in Africa.* (Bayreuth: Bayreuth African Studies Series, 1993): blurb

5 Femi Abodunrin, *Blackness: Culture, Ideology and Discourse.* (Bayreuth: Bayreuth African Studies Series, 1996)

*Land Ownership in Tanzania,*[6] edited by Robert Debusman and Stefan Arnold, is the product of a postgraduate programme on "Inter-cultural Relations in Africa." Cecilia Namulondo Nganda's *Primary Education and Social Integration: Ethnic Stereotypes in Uganda,*[7] Ernest Beyazara's*Contemporary Relativism with Special Reference to Culture and Africa,*[8] and Rugatiri Mekacha's *The Sociolinguistic Impact of Kiswahili on Ethnic Community Languages in Tanzania: A Case Study of Ekinata*[9] each represents an outstanding example of products of the University's doctoral programme in Education, Philosophy, and African Languages, respectively. *New Religious Movement and Society in Nigeria,*[10] edited by Gudrum Ludwar-Ene, is the result of a research cooperation between certain Nigerian Religious Studies scholars and the Department of Religious Studies of Bayreuth University. And, as a final example, Iwalewa Haus had, between December 1984 and February 1985, invited Twins Seven Seven, the Nigerian multi-talented artist, to Sydney, Australia, where he was able to carry out extensive conversations with Ulli Beier, then the director of the Haus. The conversations were subsequently edited by Beier himself and reconstructed into an autobiography. It has now been published by BASS under the title *A Dreaming life: an Autobiography of Twins Seven Seven.*[11]

## V

As already pointed out, the second group of publications under BASS are made up of the results of the research initiatives of Eckhard Breitinger himself. To be sure, there always exists a danger when an editor/publisher employs his/her outfit to push out his/her own works. Such a situation tends to encourage, on the part of the editor/publisher, complacency, mediocrity, or, worse still, incest. It would, however, appear that in his own case, Breitinger has, relatively, been able to successfully – at least so far – skirt the borderlines of these dangers. For one, the man has remained a consistent and regular contributor to most of the major journals as well as special publications in his field, even in spite of BASS. Second, he

6 Robert Debusman & Stefan Arnold, *Land, Law and Land Ownership in Tanzania.* (Bayreuth African Studies Series, 1996)

7 Cecilia Namlondo Nganda, *Primary Education and Social Integration: Ethnic Stereotypes in Uganda.* (Bayreuth African Studies Series, 1994)

8 Ernest Beyazara, *Contemporary Relativism with Special Reference to Culture and Africa.* (Bayreuth: Bayreuth African Studies Series, 1994)

9 Rugatiri Mekacha, *The Sociolinguistic Impact of Kiswahili on Ethnic Community Languages in Tanzania: A Case Study of Ekinata.* (Bayreuth: Bayreuth African Studies Series, 1993)

10 Gudrun Ludwar – Ene, ed. *New Religious Movement and Society in Nigeria.* (Bayreuth: Bayreuth African Studies Series,1991)

11 Beier, Ulli ed., *A Dreaming Life: an Autobiography of Twins Seven Seven.* (Bayreuth: Bayreuth African Studies Series,1999)

has also edited a number of books which have been handled by other publishing outfits. [12] Finally, as can be seen, *Anglophone Cameroon Writing*, [13] the first book that Breitinger did for the series, is volume 30 and it came out in 1993 nearly ten years after the birth of the series, while *Uganda: The Cultural Landscape*, [14] the second, is number 39, coming out another five years later. Clearly not many editors/publishers who themselves are writers and scholars have been known to have been able to exercise this kind of reticence.

Objectively, it would seem then that Breitinger's projects that have appeared in African Studies Series are those that, given their nature, must inevitably be handled by the series; or – and this is more or less putting the same point differently – that they are those that have the same relationship with Bayreuth University as those in the first category. Honesty, at least in my own view, demands, however, that they be treated separately.

Incidentally, *Anglophone Cameroon Writing*, Breitinger's first contribution to the series, represents the one that I also take as the first example. Jointly edited by Nalova Lyonga, Eckhard Breitinger and Bole Botake, the book represents the first full-length publication on Anglophone writing in Cameroon; and it was itself the culmination of a series of events which included a high-powered conference hosted by the Goethe Institute, Yaounde, and which was attended by both the British and German ambassadors to Cameroon.

Truly, Anglophone Cameroon literature had for a very long time remained neglected. In fact, and as stated in the foreword to the book, the literature had been seriously denigrated [15] until 1993 when the conference took place. The event thus became a groundbreaking activity powered with the aim of properly defining the status of Anglophone Cameroon writing, of attracting attention to it, of further promoting its growth and of encouraging critical interest in it. The three editors of the book write regarding the objective of the conference:

---

12 To cite just one example, Breitinger edited *Defining New Idioms and Alternative Forms of Expression*, being the proceedings of the 1995 conference of the German association of New English Literatures (ASNEL). See Ekhard Breitinger ed., *Defining New Idioms and Alternative Forms of Expression*. (Amsterdam: Rodopi Cross Cultures, 1996)

13 Nalova Lyonga, Eckhard Breitinger & Bole Botake, eds., *Anglophone Cameroon Writing*. (Bayreuth: Bayreuth African Studies Series, 1993)

14 Eckhard Breitinger, ed., *Uganda: The Cultural Landscape*. (Bayreuth: Bayreuth African Studies Series,1999)

15 In *The African Quest for Freedom and Identity: Cameroon Writing and the National Experience*, Richard Bjornson writes "On an international level, scholars and critics tended to regard Cameroon writing primarily within the context of Francophone African literature." The implication of this statement is that Anglophone writing either does not exist or is too insignificant to merit separate attention. See Richard Bjornson, *The African Quest for Freedom and Identity: Cameroon Writing and the National Experience*. (Bloomington/Indianapolis: Indiana University Press, 1991): 303

> The workshop had to take stock of the corpus and volume of Anglophone Cameroon writing, assess its standing, evaluate and redefine its status and its functions in the present situation: This meant that participants analyze Anglophone writing in relation to, or in contrast with, Francophone writing in Cameroon and other Anglophone writing in Africa and throughout the World. The workshop was also to serve as a first step toward creating viable structures to enhance the production, the promulgation and the criticism of Anglophone Cameroon writing.[16]

Going by the editors' claim, the aim of the published proceedings is "to serve as a reference; as a base on which future critical discourse in the field can focus."[17] Perhaps because of the nature of the project as a pioneering activity, the organizers were liberal in their definition of what constitutes literature. Presentations were thus included in the published proceedings on such topics as "Pre-Independence Evolution of Western Education in Anglophone Cameroon,' 'Anglophone Cameroon Writing in Relation to Textbooks in Cameroon Schools,' and 'The Role of the Newspapers in the Democratic Process in Cameroon." But, on the whole, what the publication seeks to emphasize is the role of literature in the process of inventing the cultural identity of the people of Anglophone Cameroon, and it certainly discharges this task creditably well. There were papers which articulate the definition of the literature, which explore its oral heritage, and which eventually study its written production. The deficiency of the literature especially in the area of prose narratives is frankly admitted.

Sponsored jointly by a consortium of German institutions, including the German Embassy in Cameroon, the Goethe Institute, Yaounde, the Deutsche Forschungsgemeinschaft, and the Deutsche Akademischer Austauschdienst (DAAD), the conference falls neatly under the "Identity in Africa" programme. Only BASS, it seems, could have handled the publication of its proceedings.

Almost exactly the same statement can be made with respect to *Uganda: The Cultural Landscape*, published in 1999 as Bayreuth African Studies Series number 39. Uganda was arguably the cultural headquarters of East Africa in the sixties, what with the highly reputable Makerere University, the Ugandan National Theatre, and the National Museum, all located in Kampala. The country was, however, overtaken by a terrible political turmoil during the regimes of Milton Obote and, particularly, that of Idi Amin, with the latter actually perpetrating a terrible form of anti-intellectualism: censoring, harassing, and assassinating artists, cultural workers, and intellectuals in general. Under this kind of situation, it is natural that cultural activity would be brought to a standstill. Those artists and writers who continued to work did so under very suicidal conditions. The late Robert Serumaga for example, as Breitinger points out in the introduction to *Uganda: the*

[16] *Anglophone Cameroon Writing*, 10

[17] *Anglophone Cameroon Writing*, 12

*Cultural Landscape*, "deliberately avoided scripting or video-recording his plays to evade the wrath of the powerful." And several others followed in his footsteps, "partly for political reasons, (and) partly for sheer want of materials":

> Thus the years of turmoil also resulted in a tremendous loss of knowledge about Ugandan culture due to lack of proper documentation. Play scripts were lost or destroyed, the script documentation with the National Theatre is less than satisfactory for those years (1970–85), photographs of productions were not systematically collected, and tapes of recordings with Radio Uganda were wiped out owing to lack of blank tapes. Relatively little is today accessible on an ordered systematic archival level. [18]

It was against this background that Eckhard Breitinger, seizing on the opportunity of relative freedom that now operated in the country, embarked on a project designed to document, comprehensively, Uganda's cultural development from the colonial times right through to the 1990s. But the German teacher of African literature was wrong in presuming that the project would be as smooth-sailing as the one on Anglophone Cameroon writing. Well, there probably is a second basis for his optimism. Because he had also successfully collaborated with Rose Mbowa, formerly head of Music, Dance and Drama at Makerere University, on a project on theatre for development sponsored jointly by the German Ministry for Technical Cooperation and Kabarole Basic Health Project and there had been no problem with the project right from the beginning to the publication stage.

But to go on, after a series of preliminary contacts and deliberations, the first meeting of would-be contributors was held in Makerere University in 1994. Here participants deliberated on the scope of the project and assigned chapters to writers. But the plans did not progress as had been laid out. "Contributions came in hesitantly," says Breitinger, as "some of the contributors withdrew form the project, others just failed to deliver their articles." [19] And it was not always easy to find replacements. But what emerged eventually, according to the editor, still represents a close approximation of the original conception. To be sure, contributions covered almost all aspects of Uganda's cultural life. There were chapters on the publishing industry, on Makerere University itself, and on its well-known experimental theatre model, the Free Traveling Theatre. Other sections are on oral and written traditions, poetry, prose narratives, drama and theatre, and the visual arts. Contributors were mainly from Uganda but there also were included such foreigners as David Cook and Rose-Marie Rycher both of whom, without doubt, had been intensely involved in Uganda's cultural history in the recent past. It is

[18] Eckhard Breitinger ed. *Uganda: The Cultural Landscape.* (Bayreuth: Bayreuth African Studies Series, 1999): 13

[19] *Uganda: The Cultural Landscape*, 7

perhaps a measure of the book's acceptability in the country that it has now been re-issued by Fountain Publishers, Uganda's largest publishing outfit.

Three more books either edited or co-edited by Breitinger were published under the series. But the pattern is similar. Either the book represents the outcome of a project sponsored under the "Identity in Africa" programme or it could distinctly be categorized under the Bayreuth African Studies programme. *Theatre and Performance in Africa: Inter-cultural Perspectives* [20] arose out of a conference held at the University of Bayreuth in 1992 focusing on the theme "Defining New idioms and Alternative Forms of Expression in African Theatre." *Theatre for Development* [21], published back-to-back in English and French, has been cited earlier. It was the product of a collaborative effort between Eckhard Breitinger and Rose Mbowa, on the one hand, and the German Ministry for Technical Cooperation and the Kabarole Basic Health project, on the other. The levels of cooperation that produced *History and Theatre in Africa,* [22] which Breitinger co-edited with Yvonne Hutchinson, was equally multi-faceted. Simultaneously labelled as a special edition of *South African Theatre Journal* (SAT), the book, as Breitinger suggests, "marks the beginning of cooperation between the two Arts Faculties of the Universities of Stellenbosch and Bayreuth":

> It is also an experiment of joining the publications of both institutions on a particular topic of common research interests, i.e. the history of theatre and the representation of history in theatre. It is an attempt to cast the net wider for the two publications and bring our publications to the attention of the respective customers and subscribers and thereby broaden the distribution and international presence of both publications. [23]

It seems such a nice idea, and it may be necessary for BASS to, as a matter of urgency, consider more of such initiatives if it were to achieve its aim of establishing a real presence in Africa. But more on this later.

## VI

None of the publications under the third category of BASS output have any prior relationship with Bayreuth University. Rather, and as pointed out earlier, each of the manuscripts emerged as an independent submission by its author to the

---

20 Eckhard Breitinger, (ed.) *Theatre and Performance in Africa: Intercultural Perspectives.* (Bayreuth: Bayreuth African Studies Series, 1994)

21 Eckhard Breitinger, (ed.) *Theatre for Development.* (Bayreuth: Bayreuth African Studies Series,1994)

22 Yvette Hutchinson & Eckhard Breitinger (ed.) *History and Theatre in Africa.* (Bayreuth: Bayreuth African Studies Series, 2000)

23 *History and Theatre in Africa*, 5

editor/publisher. But beyond that, perhaps, is the fact that each of them represents the first full length study on the subject it engages. I cite two examples.

The first is titled *The Life and Writings of Gakara wa Wanjau*. Of the subject of the book, Christiana Pugliese, the author, writes:

> Garaka wa Wanjau is the major writer in Gikuyu. Not only is he the most prolific of Kenyan authors, but also probably a unique case in Africa of an author and a publisher in an African language whose activity has never ceased in the last fifty years. He started writing in the mid-forties and, since then, he has published a large number of booklets about Gikuyu customs, culture and language, as well as Kenyan politics and history. He has also brought out a prison diary, a novel many pieces of short fiction and several Gikuyu readers for primary school which have been included on the official syllabus. [24]

In spite of this, and a 1994 NOMA award for publishing in Africa to boot, Gakara wa Wanjau remained largely neglected. Originally submitted as a doctoral dissertation to the School of Oriental and African Studies (SOAS), University of London, *The Life and Writings of Gakara wa Wanjau* was later revised for publication with a grant from the French institute for Research in Africa (IFRA). It dwells at length on the life history of its subject, on his works in the development of Gikuyu orthography, and, in detail, on his fictional writings. BASS published the book in cooperation with IFRA.

The second example is *The Novels of Nuruddin Farah.* [25] As the title suggests, the book, written by Derek Wright, has Nuruddin Farah, the Somali writer as its subject. Author of at least eight published novels and several unpublished scripts in other genres and winner of several prizes and awards, including the Neustadt International prize for Literature, Nuruddin Farah remained unexplored at least at a sustained level by critics up until 1994 when Wright's book was first published. Jacqueline Bardolph, the woman who translated most of Farah's novel into French, attributes this to the author's isolated position – since he has lived in exile since 1974 – and the fact that some of the works were not easy to get. Reed Way Dasenbrock proposes that "the fact [that] Somalia does not provide [Farah] with a local context and readership" could be another possible explanation.

Be that as it may, the book is deliberately structured as an introductory study. Wright also thinks that "a systematic investigation of the indigenous narrative, religious and linguistic sources of Farah's fiction is a task better left to Somali and Somali-speaking scholars with first-hand knowledge of the relevant traditions." [26] The book has eight chapters, with one devoted to each of the seven novels which

---

[24] Christina Pugliese, *Author, Publisher and Gikuyu Nationalist: The life and Writings of Gakara wa Wanjau.* (Bayreuth: Bayreuth African Studies Series, 1995): 11

[25] Derek Wright, *The Novels of Nuruddin Farah.* (Bayreuth: Bayreuth African Studies Series,1994)

[26] *The Novels of Nuruddin Farah*, 2

Farah has, at that time, published. These are preceded by an introductory chapter on the writer and his background. In each of the seven major chapters, Wright proceeds by first giving a summary of the story, followed by a sensitive analysis of the themes, and then a discussion of the socio-political background; ending, ultimately, with critical notes on the particular novel being discussed. Wright, who has also authored books on Soyinka and Armah, also makes occasional forays into technical criticism, especially in those novels where Farah himself betrays postmodernist influences. Examples include *Maps* and *Gifts*, the first two parts of the nomadic writer's second trilogy. As far as it goes (Wright leaves out Farah's non-fictive writings, his unpublished plays, and his short novel written in Somali), the book tackles its subject quite adequately. Wright proves himself to be a hard-nosed reader and a very neat writer, and reviewers have in turn hailed his work as an "excellent, insightful, introduction to Farah's work." [27]

## VII

The Bayreuth African Studies Series has surely come a long way. The series now seems to have been accepted in the academies of the North. This is attested to by the regular subscriptions maintained by the libraries of several institutions in the United States, Britain, France, Sweden, Belgium, Denmark, Austria, The Netherlands, Italy, and of course Germany. The books also sell fairly well in conferences organized by learned societies of relevant disciplines. These include respective African Studies Associations of America and several European countries, the US-based African Literature Association (ALA) and Germany's Association of New English Literature (ASNEL).

Another measure of BASS' success lies in the quality of review its publications have been receiving. I have earlier cited what *West Africa* has to say about *The Novels of Nuruddin Farah. Research in African Literature*, arguably the most authoritative journal currently in African Literature, considers the same book as an "inspired piece of in-depth interpretation" [28]

In its review of *Theatre and Performance in Africa: Intercultural Perspectives, Theatre Research International* holds that Eckhard Breitinger "has brought together contributions that form an important resource for all concerned with African theatre" [29]. In *Musical Opinion, Yoruba Drumming: The Dundun Tradi-*

---

27 Chris Dunton, "A Gift from Somalia: *The Novels of Nuruddin Farah* by Derek Wright" *West Africa*. (Aug. 22–28, 1994): 1489

28 Jacqueline Bardolph, "A Review of *The Novels of Nuruddin Farah. Research in African Literature,* Vol. 26, 2, 225

29 Martin Banham, "A Review of *Theatre and Performance in Africa: Intercultural Perspectives* Edited by Eckhard Breitinger." *Theatre Research International* Vol. 20,2: 173

*tion,* [30] the revised doctoral thesis of Akin Euba published as series number 21/22, is recommended as a "well-rounded study, full of information on the history of [Yoruba] music and instruments, the training of musicians, performing techniques, and the religious and secular uses of *dundun.*" [31] As a final example, Ahonagnon Noel Gbaguidi's *Erbrecht an Grund und Boden in Benin: Betrachtungen zur Ermittlung des Rebstatus in einem Mehrrechtstaat,* a book on law written in German, is hailed by the *Journal of Legal Pluralism and Unofficial Law* as a "detailed, incisively argued study of a plural, and consequently complex area of state law." [32] This last example should draw attention also to a point which earlier has been touched upon but which needs to be fully re-stated. And this is the fact that though the majority of its titles are in English, BASS also publishes books written in other major European languages, notably French and German.

But the foregoing is not to suggest that Bayreuth African Studies publications are of even standard. No. Because, to put it bluntly, a number of the titles in the series are of questionable quality. I cite just two examples, each at a different extreme of deficiency. The first is Olu Obafemi's *Contemporary Nigerian Theatre: Cultural Heritage and Social Vision,* [33] which is supposed to be a re-working of a doctoral dissertation submitted to the University of Leeds in 1981. At the time that the thesis was first submitted, it came out as an original piece of work, almost of a landmark proportion. However, by the time it was published as a book in 1996, the work had become clearly outdated, what with the numerous plays staged and published during the fifteen-year gap and the innumerable work of criticism produced on them. Obafemi himself has published at least nine essays from the thesis. One of them, "Revolutionary Aesthetics in Recent Nigerian Theatre," which came out in *African Literature Today* Volume 12 in 1982, has been cited and re-cited by different critics of Nigerian drama. In proposing it for publication at least fifteen years after it was first written, therefore, one expected Obafemi to have undertaken a thorough and rigorous revision of the dissertation. But this was not the case. Indeed, what has been presented to scholars of Nigerian drama and theatre in 1996 is hardly different from what Obafemi submitted to his examiners in 1981. To be sure, Breitinger himself did not seem to be too impressed by what the professor of dramatic literature at the University of Ilorin, Nigeria, submitted to him. According to him, Breitinger that is, the original understanding

---

[30] Akin Euba, *Yoruba Drumming: The Dundun Tradition.* (Bayreuth African Studies Series, 1990)

[31] Anonymous, "A Review of *Yoruba Drumming: The Dundun Tradition* by Akin Euba." *Musical Opinion* No 1371, Vol. 115,: 126

[32] Gordon R. Woodman, "Ahonagnon Noel Gbaguidi, *Erbrecht an Grund und Boden in Benin: Betrachtungen zur Ermittlung des Erbstatuts in einem Mehrrechstaat.*" *Journal of Legal Pluralism and Unofficial Law,* No 40 186

[33] Olu Obafemi, *Contemporary Nigerian Theatre: Cultural Heritage and Social Vision.* (Bayreuth: Bayreuth African Studies Series, 1996)

reached with Obafemi was that he should revise and update the script substantially, but Obafemi's revisions, however, turned out to be much less substantial than he thought was absolutely necessary.

The second example is Ezenwa-Ohaeto's *Contemporary Nigerian Poetry and the Poetics of Orality*[34]. Judging both from the pattern of selection of materials and the order of their arrangement it would appear that this book was rushed, indeed that the author never had much time to think through his ideas. Beside this is the level of analysis, which also seems to fall below expectation, and the quality of expression, which may be regarded as inelegant. This view is corroborated by James Gibbs in his review of the book in *World Literature Today*, a United States of America-based journal. He comments, inter-alia, on the book:

> The scope of the volume, the quality of the writing, and the construction of the argument are deficient. The quotations from the first page of the book that I incorporated into my opening paragraph are symptomatic of the stylistic clumsiness which marks much that follows... A critical analysis that moves, as Ezenwa-Ohaeto does, into the troubled area of style must be presented in opaque prose that does not draw attention to itself-and this cannot be said for the manner in which *Contemporary Nigerian Poetry* is written.[35]

That Breitinger has had to issue this book was, I suspect, a consequence of a fundamental difficulty which still confronts his publication outfit. I discuss this straightaway.

## VIII

In spite of the wide acceptance of its publications, BASS still remains a small publishing outfit with no solid financial base. Breitinger himself often readily admits the vulnerability of the venture. Because of this problem, he has been very shrewd in the way he manages the outfit. Right now, there is absolutely no structure. For several years, the outfit was run by only one man, Breitinger, and it was not until in the past two or three years, that Pia Thielman, his wife came on board to join him as a co-publisher/editor. Actually, the latter's name appears first on the editor/publisher's page in the titles they have issued in recent time. To the best of my knowledge, the duo – or rather Breitinger, since he ran it single – handedly for a long time – do not reckon with overhead in calculating the production cost, or with man-hours since they personally edit and prepare the manuscripts using their private time; and with running costs since they also use their private transport to do the running around. The average number of issues per year stands at

[34] Ezenwa Ohaeto, *Contemporary Nigerian Poetry and the Poetics of Orality.* (Bayreuth: Bayreuth African Studies Series, 1998)

[35] James Gibbs, "Ezenwa Ohaeto: *Contemporary Nigerian Poetry and the Poetics of Orality.*" *World Literature Today*. (Spring, 1995): 35

between three and four titles, while the average print run per publication is five hundred. The standard practice is to wait after a volume has been published until enough sales have been recorded before proceeding on the next issue. It probably ought to be added though that of recent, the series has depended more on assistance and sponsorship from agencies and foundations in pushing out many of its titles. *History and Theatre in Africa* was, for example, published with assistance jointly from the University of Bayreuth and the German Academic Exchange Service, (DAAD); *Theatre for Development* was financed by the German Ministry for Technical Cooperation; while *The Life and Writings of Gakara wa Wanjau* was supported by IFRA, Nairobi. Ezenwa Ohaeto's *Contemporary Nigerian Poetry and the Poetics of Orality* represents the product of the research carried out by the author while he was an Alexander von Humboldt research fellow in Bayreuth between 1994 and 1995. Its publication was therefore sponsored by the Humboldt Foundation.

Another problem confronting BASS is how to get its publications distributed in institutions located in Africa where, even as the editor/publisher admits, they are most needed. Breitinger has adopted a two-pronged approach in an attempt to tackle this problem. The first is the joint publication agreements that he has been signing with a number of African publishers and research agencies. I have earlier cited the example of *History and Theatre in Africa* which was published jointly with the *South African Theatre Journal* (SAT). Beside this, *Uganda: The Cultural Landscape*, again as has been stated, has been published by Fountain Publishers, Uganda, Omojola's *Nigerian Art Music* and Pugliese's *The Life and Writings of Gakaara wa Wanjau* were published in cooperation with IFRA in Ibadan and Nairobi respectively, *Yoruba Drumming: The Dundun Tradition* was issued jointly with Elekoto Music Centre, Lagos, while, as a final example, *Anglophone Cameroon Writing* was produced in cooperation with *WEKA – A Journal of Anglophone Cameroon Writing and the Arts*. The African –based publishers are supposed to handle the circulation of the books in their respective localities. It must be added, however, that only a few of the titles have been so jointly produced, and Breitinger may need to put in a little more effort in this regard.

The details of the second approach are contained in a flyer which BASS started circulating a few years back. And, directly, it is a remedial scheme being proposed to willing donors of books to African institutions. For this scheme, BASS offers all its titles at a discount of 30% in addition to a tax deductible invoice. Once a prospective donor makes the necessary payment and furnishes the series with information on the name and address of the benefiting library as well as the name of the librarian in charge, BASS takes full responsibility for the shipping of the books. Not a bad proposal, certainly, though it does not appear as if the initiative has received a particularly enthusiastic response.

# IX

But it will be very unfortunate if the impression is created, whether deliberately or inadvertently, that Breitinger's initiative, or even the Africa Studies programme of Bayreuth University represents the first instance of sustained German interest in African Studies. Breitinger certainly has a number of predecessors, and also a few contemporaries; and some of them are actually qualified to be described as having plunged fully into, and even dissolved themselves in, African Cultural Studies. Some of them are indeed pioneers, and their contributions have gone a long way in helping to define the discipline.

The first person to come to mind in this regard is Janheinz Jahn, the author of *Muntu: A History of Neo-African Culture*,[36] a ground-breaking work which was first published in 1958. Another example is Ulli Beier, who first arrived in Nigeria in 1950 to take up a position as a lecturer in English Phonetics at the newly established University of Ibadan but who ultimately veered off into Yoruba cultural studies. Finally, there is Wilfred Feuser, described by Femi Ojo-Ade as a "Nigerian accidentally born in Germany." Feuser spent almost forty years in Nigeria teaching and researching Francophone and Lusophone African literatures. Among Breitinger's contemporaries are Geofferey V. Davies and Frank Schulze – Engler, the joint editors of the *Rodopi: Cross Culture* series. There also is Holger G. Ehling, initiator and founder of *Matatu: A Journal of African Culture and Society*, which started off in 1987 and which produced six editions before merging in 1990 with Editions Rodopi B.V, an Amsterdam-based publishing venture.[37] Last is Rudiger Koppe who runs a publishing outfit in Cologne dedicated mainly to African languages and linguistics.

To be able to properly mark out Breitinger's place within the German tradition of scholarship in African studies, it may be necessary to sketch an outline of the achievement of those who have been identified as his predecessors.

The fire of Janheinz Jahn's interest in African literature and culture was first kindled when in 1952 he met Leopold Sedar Senghor who, as a member of French Parliament, had come to deliver a lecture on African cultural heritage in Frankfurt. Following a talk he had afterwards with the man who was later to become the president of Senegal, Jahn had immediately commenced an intense research into African and West Indian literatures and cultures, publishing his first article on the

[36] Jahnheinz Jahn, *Muntu: A History of Neo-African Culture*. (London: Faber & Faber, 1961)

[37] In *Matatu* number 7, the first edition of the journal handled by Rodopi, the decision to merge the journal with the Amsterdam- based publishing outfit is explained in the following words: "This step had to be taken to ensure the continued existence of the journal. *Matatu* is not linked to any institution and always had to find the means to finance production. We were not sure whether we would be able to maintain a certain standard of quality all our own." See *Matatu* Number 7. (1990): iv

subject the same year. Within a few more years, Jahn had become an expert in the field, publishing articles, giving talks, editing anthologies, and translating works of authors from Africa, the Caribbean, and America into German. He coined the term "Neo-African literature", as Bernth Lindfors says, in order "to distinguish the new writing emerging in the black world from the traditional oral literature which many Europeans still presumed to bc the only mode of literary expression utilized by black people." [38]

Jahn met Ulli Beier at the first World Black Writers congress held in Paris in 1956, and the two immediately concluded arrangements to found *Black Orpheus,* the first journal of African literature. In 1958, *Muntu: An Outline of Neo-African Culture* was published. Muntu was an intensely controversial but nonetheless highly successful book. Within three years, it had been translated into seven European languages, including English, French, Dutch, and Italian. Janheinz Jahn was simply a restless spirit whose thirst for knowledge and information on African peoples' life and culture could not be satiated. From the moment he first encountered Senghor, he never for once looked back. He was always travelling, always exploring, always giving talks and lectures, always writing, transcribing, editing, and compiling anthologies and bibliographical references. By the time he died at the age of fifty-five in 1973, he had pushed out fifty-four books, over eighty essays and articles, and yet another fifty radio talks and essays.

Ulli Beier's output is equally prodigious. Yet, when he first set out from Britain to take up his appointment in 1950, he knew very little about Africa, and even much less about Nigeria and her peoples. With his transfer from English to the Extra-mural Studies Department of the University, where from 1951 he served as regional tutor for Western Nigeria, Beier had an opportunity to relocate from Ibadan to any other place within the region. Between 1951 and 1954 he was in Ede, where he organized the first Summer Conference on Yoruba Culture and co-launched *Odu*, a journal of Yoruba studies, together with Saburi Biobaku. Beier was in Ilobu between 1954 and 1958, and in Osogbo from that time until he left Nigeria in December 1966.

Though the contributions of Janheinz Jahn to the take – off of *Black Orpheus* were very important, the real credit for the success of the journal should be taken by Ulli Beier. *Black Orpheus* was the journal that first published the works of virtually all Nigerian pioneer writers of English expression, and this includes Wole Soyinka, J.P. Clark, and Christopher Okigbo. More or less an extension of that journal, or vice-versa, was the Mbari club, a socio-cultural and intellectual organization which was founded in March 1961. Mbari, also a brain-child of Beier,

[38] Bernth Lindfors, "The Works of Jahnheinz Jahn." In *Neo-African Literature and Culture" Essays in Memory of Jahnheinz Jahn* (Mainz: Mainzer Afrika – Studien, 1976): 13

had a gallery in which traditional and tradition-inspired works of art were exhibited, a stage on which new plays, including J.P. Clark's *Song of a Goat* and Wole Soyinka's *The Trials of Brother Jero* were first mounted, and a publishing wing which produced twenty-four books of original African writing in two years. Ulli Beier returned to Nigeria for another three years in 1971 to serve, this time, as the Director of the Institute of African Studies of the University of Ife (now Obafemi Awolowo University). An opportunity for him to continue his work in Germany presented itself when he was appointed as the first Director of Iwalewa Haus, earlier described as the Africa Centre of the University of Bayreuth. Beier held this position twice, first between 1981 and 1984 and later between 1989 and 1996. In terms of scholarship, Beier's output is no less astounding. Wole Ogundele actually listed over two hundred critical and creative books, monographs, essays and articles, anthologies, interviews, translations, and biographical works for Ulli Beier in the select bibliography included in *Omoluabi: Ulli Beier, Yoruba Society and Culture*,[39] his definitive biography of the man.

In "In Memoriam of Prof. Willfried Feuser, Best of Friends: 1928 – 2000," Gerald Moser describes Willfried Feuser as "a man of many talents and interests, a writer of penetrating book reviews, articles, essays and anthologies and an outstanding educator."[40] Feuser left for Nigeria as soon as he completed his doctoral work in Comparative Literature at the University of Freiburg in 1960. After a brief stop-over at the University of Ibadan, he transferred to the University of Ife (now Obafemi Awolowo University) where for several years he served as Head of the Department of Modern European Languages. He designed and taught courses in French, German, and Portuguese languages and cultures, and also in Francophone, Lusophone, and Germanophone African writings. He continued precisely with the same thing even when he moved to the University of Port-Harcourt in 1978. His cornucopia of books, articles, essays, and anthologies is published in different languages, including English, German, Portuguese, French, and Dutch, Feuser returned to Germany on his retirement in 1996, but, having taken a Nigerian identity, he never felt at home again in his country of birth. As his illness worsened, he was returned to Nigeria in 1999. There he died and was buried in 2000.

---

[39] Wole Ogundele, Omoluabi: *Ulli Beier, Yoruba Society and Culture*. (Bayreuth: Bayreuth African Studies Series, 2003)

[40] Gerald Moser, "In Memoriam of Prof. Willfried Feuser: Best of Friends: 1928 – 2000." *ALA Bulletin* (Summer 2000): 78

# X

Now, if Jahn, Beier, and Feuser were pioneers who helped to define the discipline of African Studies, Breitinger stands shoulder high among those who are further exploring the field, who are breaking new ground, and who are advancing the frontiers of the subject. Jahn never held a regular job. Breitinger does, and has continued to teach and supervise students in the area. He has also published widely in the field, having churned out over a hundred books, articles, translations, reviews, etc. Unlike Beier and Feuser, Breitinger has never stayed for a really long stretch in Africa. He is based mainly in Germany, preferring short, sporadic research and teaching visits to different countries on the continent and in different parts of her Diaspora. In spite of this, his knowledge of Africa and her peoples is no less profound. The man has also converted his being located in the homeland into another advantage as he has continued to play host to different scholars and researchers from Africa, as well as, in different areas of African Studies.

Through *Black Orpheus,* Janheinz Jahn and Ulli Beier initiated the first platform through which people could express critical opinions on the new literature. With BASS, Breitinger is carrying those efforts further. Such efforts are of particular importance now because, owing to the way neo-colonialism/neo-imperialism has been played out in Africa, the continent has been ravaged and devastated by war, famine, and debts. Under such circumstances it is logical that cultural and intellectual developments and endeavours will become casualties. But through his small outfit, Breitinger has been able to provide an opportunity to a number of people who otherwise might never have been heard; has helped to direct attention to unexplored literatures, contributed to efforts on cultural reconstruction in war-ravaged zones, and has been able to, finally, inspire sustained studies of certain neglected writers. Even if in a limited sense, the man can, because of this, be described as an ambassador of hope.

Initially, the Bayreuth African Studies Series had entailed enormous sacrifice on the part of the editor/publisher, especially in terms of time and energy, and it is certainly admirable how he was able to cope and to surmount the numerous obstacles he encountered over the years. Now, having retired from the University of Bayreuth, the outfit seems to have become the major business with which both Breitinger and his wife, Pia Thielman, are pre-occupied. It also probably is their major source of livelihood. This may be in order, at least for now. It is doubtful if the same thing can be said for the project in the long term. The point, if it can be put directly, is that even a family business ought to have a structure. It is indeed necessary, in my view, to work out proper method of entering into contractual agreement with would – be authors, to have a procedure for receiving and processing manuscripts and to have a standardized mode of distributing and/or marketing publications. One makes these recommendations directly out of a concern for the long term existence of the venture. Because, it will be clearly sad if, at the end day, such a project has to terminate either as a consequence of lack of finance or because, for one reason or the other, either or both of the two people responsible for keeping it going now can no longer carry on.

## WORKS CITED

Abdul-Jalil, Musa: "The Dynamics of Ethnic Identification in Northern Darfur: a Situational Approach" *Bayreuth African Studies Series*, Vol. 1, 1984 55 – 85.

Abodunrin, Femi: *Blackness: Culture, Ideology and Discourse*. (Bayreuth: Bayreuth African Studies Series, 1996).

Aguda, Akinola: "The Machinery of Justice and the Training and Appointment of Judges in Nigeria" (Bayreuth: Bayreuth African Studies Series, Vol. 11, 1989): 5 – 24.

Anonymous. "Yoruba Drumming: the Dundun Tradition by Akin Euba" *Musical Opinion* (No 1371, Vol. 115. March 1992): 126.

Banham, Martin: "A Review of *Theatre and Performance in Africa: Intercultural Perspectives* Edited by Eckhard Breitinger" in *Theatre Research International* (Vol. 20, No 2, Summer 1995): 172 – 173.

Barber, Karin: "Radical Conservation in Yoruba Popular Plays" in *Bayreuth African Studies Series*, Vol. 7 1986 5 – 32.

Bardolph, Jacqueline: "A Review of *The Novels of Nuruddin Farah" in Research in African Literature*, (Vol. 26, No 2, Summer 95): 225 – 227.

Bashir, Omah Mohammed: "Ethnicity, Regionalism and National Cohesion in the Sudan" in *Bayreuth African Studies Series*, Vol. 1 1984 5 – 37.

Beier, Ulli (ed.): *A Dreaming Life: an Autobiography of Twins Seven Seven*. (Bayreuth: Bayreuth African Studies Series, 1999).

Beyazara, Ernest: *Contemporary Relativism with Special Reference to Culture and Africa*. (Bayreuth: Bayreuth African Studies Series, 1994).

Breitinger, Eckhard (ed.): *Theatre and Performance in Africa: Intercultural Perspectives*. (Bayreuth: Bayreuth African Studies Series, 1994).

Breitinger, Eckhard (ed.) *Theatre for Development*. (Bayreuth: Bayreuth African Studies, 1994).

Breitinger, Eckhard (ed.) *Uganda: the Cultural Landscape*. (Bayreuth: Bayreuth African Studies Series, 1999).

Debusman, Robert & Arnold, Stefan (ed.): *Land Law and Land Ownership in Tanzania*. (Bayreuth: Bayreuth African Studies Series, 1996).

Doi, Abdur-Rahman: "The Impact of English Law Concepts on the Administration of Islamic law in Nigeria" in *Bayreuth African Studies Series* Vol. 11, 1989 25 – 56.

Dunton, Chris. "A Gift from Somalia: *The Novels of Nuruddin Farah* by Derek Wright." In *West Africa* (23 – 28 August, 1994): 1489.

Euba, Akin. *Essays on Music in Africa 2: Intercultural Perspectives*. (Bayreuth: Bayreuth African Studies Series, 1989).

Euba, Akin. *Yoruba Drumming: The Dundun Tradition.* (Bayreuth: Bayreuth African Studies Series, 1990).

Gbaguidi, Noel. *Erbrecht an Grund und Boden in Benin: Betrachtungen zur Ermittlung des Rebstatus in einem Mehrrectstaat.* (Bayreuth: Bayreuth African Studies Series, 1994).

Gibbs James. "Ezenwa-Ohaeto: *Contemporary Nigerian Poetry and the Poetics of Orality.*" In *World Literature Today.* (Spring 1999).

Hutchinson, Yvette & Breitinger, Eckhard (eds.). *History and Theatre in Africa* (Bayreuth: Bayreuth African Studies Series, 2000).

Jahn, Janheinz. *Muntu: An Outline of Neo-African Culture.* (London: Faber & Faber, 1961).

John, Alex. "The Development of Sierra Leone Krio." *Bayreuth African studies vol.* 2 69 – 106.

Lindfors, Bernth. "The Works of Janheinz Jahn" in *Neo-African Literature and Culture: Essays in Memory of Janheinz Jahn* edited by Bernth Lindfors & Ulla Schild. (Mainz: Mainzer Afrika-Studien, 1976): 10 – 23.

Ludwar-Ene Gudrun. *New Religious Movement in Nigeria.* (Bayreuth: Bayreuth African Studies Series, 1991).

Ludwar-Ene Gudrun & Reh Mechthild (ed.): *Focus on Women in Africa,* (Bayreuth: Bayreuth Africa Studies Series, 1993).

Lyonga Nalova, Breitinger, Eckhard & Botake, Bole (ed.) *Anglophone Cameroon Writing.* (Bayreuth: Bayreuth African Studies Series, 1993).

Mekacha, Rugatiri:*The Socio-Linguistic Impact of Kiswahili on Ethnic Community Languages in Tanzania: A Case Study of Ekinata.* (Bayreuth: Bayreuth African Studies Series, 1993).

Mohammed-Salih, A.R. Mohammed "National vs Regional: Some Methodological problems in the study of Nationalism and Nation-Building in the Sudan" *Bayreuth African Studies Series* vol. 1 1984. 39 – 53.

Moser, Gerald. "In Memorian of Prof. Willfried Feuser: Best of Friends – 1928 – 2000" in*ALA Bulletin,* (Summer 2000. 71 – 78).

Mganda Namulondo. *Primary Education and Social Integration: Ethnic Stereotypes in Uganda Basic Text Books.* (Bayreuth: Bayreuth African Studies Series, 1996).

Obafemi, Olu. *Contemporary Nigerian Theatre: Cultural Heritage and Social Vision.* (Bayreuth: Bayreuth African Studies Series, 1996).

Obafemi, Olu. "Revolutionary Aesthetics in Recent Nigerian Theatre" *African Literature Today* Vol. 12, 1982.

Ohaeto, Ezenwa. *Contemporary Nigerian Poetry and the Poetics of Orality.* (Bayreuth: Bayreuth African Studies Series, 1998).

Ogundele, Wole. *Omoluabi: Ulli Beier, Yoruba Society and Culture*. (Bayreuth: Bayreuth African Studies Series, 2003)

Ojo-Ade, Femi. "Memories of Feuser, a Nigerian Accidentally Born in Germany" *ALA Bulletin*. Spring. 2000. 35 – 40.

Omojola, Bode. *Nigerian Art Music*. (Bayreuth: Bayreuth African Studies Series, 1997).

Pugliese, Christiana. *Author, Publisher and Gikuyu Nationalist: The Life and Writings of Gakaara wa Wanjau*. (Bayreuth: Bayreuth African Studies Series, 1995)

Rollins, Jack, D. "Early Twentieth Century Swahili Prose Narrative Structure and Some Aspects of Swahili Ethnicity." *Bayreuth African Studies Series*. (Vol. II 1985): 49 – 68

Schmied, Josef. *English in East and Central Africa I* (Bayreuth: Bayreuth African Studies Series, 1989)

Schmied, Josef. "English in Tanzania." (Bayreuth: Bayreuth African Studies Series). Vol. V, 1986: 63 – 114

Woodman, Gordon, R. "Ahonagnon Noel Gbaguidi, *Erbrecht an Grund und Boden in Benin: Betrachtungen zur Ermittlung des Erbstatuts in einem Mehrrechtstaat*." *Journal of Legal Pluralism and Unofficial Law*. No 40, 1998. 183 – 186

Wright, Derek. *The Novels of Nuruddin Farah*. (Bayreuth: Bayreuth African Studies Series, 1994)

**Arbeitsmaterialien zur Afrikanistik**

Fekadu Bekele, Bosena Negussie

# Deutsch – Amharisch
# Amharisch – Deutsch

Ein Wörterbuch

**የጀርመንኛ- አማርኛ- የአማርኛ- ጀርመንኛ**

**መዝገበ ቃላት**

Arbeitsmaterialien zur Afrikanistik Bd. 4

LIT

Fekadu Bekele; Bosena Negusie
**Deutsch – Amharisch/Amharisch – Deutsch**
Ein Wörterbuch

Fekadu Bekele lebt seit über zwanzig Jahren in Deutschland. Er studierte Volkswirtschaft- und promovierte in der Entwicklungsökonomie. Er arbeitete als Lehrbeauftragter an der Freien Universität Berlin -und an der Fachhochschule für Wirtschaft in Berlin. Er publizierte zahlreiche Veröffentlichungen auf dem Gebiet der Entwicklungstheorie/Entwicklungspolitik -und der Auswirkungen der Auflagenpolitik der IWF und der Welt Bank auf die wirtschaftlichen Entwicklungen der schwarzafrikanischen Länder südlich der Sahara. Bosena Negussie ist Diplom Betriebswirtin und machte als eine Zusatzausbildung zur Heilpraktikerin.

Bd. 4, 2006, 264 S., 29,90 €, br., ISBN 3-8258-9476-2

LIT Verlag Berlin – Hamburg – London – Münster – Wien – Zürich
Fresnostr. 2 48159 Münster
Tel.: 0251 / 620 32 22 – Fax: 0251 / 922 60 99
e-Mail: vertrieb@lit-verlag.de – http://www.lit-verlag.de

**Littératures des Peuples noirs / African Peoples' Literatures**

Dina Taïwé Kolyang
**Orature et littéralité**
Une perspective africaine
Combien d'oralité reste-t-il dans les recueils des contes africains, après transcription et traduction des paroles des conteurs ? Le présent ouvrage part de cette interrogation pour ouvrir une piste de réflexion sur les oralités modernes et traditionnelles, en examinant la question de la mémoire et surtout les différentes galaxies créées par l'écriture et les technologies de l'information et de la communication. Dans ce hiatus culturel, l'oralité reste une compagne fidèle de l'Africain.
Bd. 3, 2008, 96 S., 19,90 €, br., ISBN 978-3-8258-1333-8

LIT Verlag Berlin – Hamburg – London – Münster – Wien – Zürich
Fresnostr. 2 48159 Münster
Tel.: 0251 / 620 32 22 – Fax: 0251 / 922 60 99
e-Mail: vertrieb@lit-verlag.de – http://www.lit-verlag.de